A CHEF'S LAMENT
"A Private Chef Goes Public"

By
E.M. Harris

© Copyright 2005 E.M. Harris.
All rights reserved. No part of this publication may be reproduced, stored in a retrieval system, or transmitted, in any form or by any means, electronic, mechanical, photocopying, recording, or otherwise, without the written prior permission of the author.

Note for Librarians: a cataloguing record for this book that includes Dewey Decimal Classification and US Library of Congress numbers is available from the Library and Archives of Canada. The complete cataloguing record can be obtained from their online database at: www.collectionscanada.ca/amicus/index-e.html
ISBN 1-4120-5743-4

TRAFFORD

Offices in Canada, USA, Ireland and UK
This book was published *on-demand* in cooperation with Trafford Publishing. On-demand publishing is a unique process and service of making a book available for retail sale to the public taking advantage of on-demand manufacturing and Internet marketing. On-demand publishing includes promotions, retail sales, manufacturing, order fulfilment, accounting and collecting royalties on behalf of the author.

Book sales for North America and international:
Trafford Publishing, 6E–2333 Government St.,
Victoria, BC V8T 4P4 CANADA
phone 250 383 6864 (toll-free 1 888 232 4444)
fax 250 383 6804; email to orders@trafford.com
Book sales in Europe:
Trafford Publishing (UK) Ltd., Enterprise House, Wistaston Road Business Centre,
Wistaston Road, Crewe, Cheshire CW2 7RP UNITED KINGDOM
phone 01270 251 396 (local rate 0845 230 9601)
facsimile 01270 254 983; orders.uk@trafford.com
Order online at:
trafford.com/05-0641

10 9 8 7 6 5 4 3 2

A good cook is one who dispenses happiness.
… Elsa Schiaparelli

Live in each season as it passes, breathe the air, drink the drink
Taste the fruit and resign yourself to the influences of each
… Henry David Thoreau

When work is a pleasure, life is a joy! When work is duty,
Life is slavery
… Maxim Gorky

CHAPTER ONE

I think I should write some things down. My head is filled with wild and weird images that I can't seem to make go away. I had an experience a year ago and I still can't shake its effects. It made me look at my life, at what was important to me, and decide what I wanted to actually *do* with the rest of it. I wasn't in the Peace Corps, I didn't become a born-again Christian, I wasn't a survivor of a plane crash or anything like that. Nope. I was simply a private chef to one of the richest couples in my city (a major metropolitan city, but for the sake of the innocent and for the sake of me not being sued I shall not name names). I saw things that, had I not been there, I would never believe to be true. I saw such excess that I still feel chilled when I think about what they had and what so many people don't have. I was subjected to prejudice and pretense the likes of which made me question my worthiness as a human being. I had always been a little cocky, maybe even a bit unbearable to some people during my life. However, no matter how much confidence I started out with, by the end of my one-year tenure as a working stiff in the bizarro real world of the rich and powerful, that bravado had been all but shattered.

So let me take you back before I get ahead of myself. It was the evening before a crucial job interview. I was sipping on a beer and going over some old menus, just biding my time. In spite of nailing a majority of interviews, I always dreaded the interview process. I truly believe the whole procedure is a huge crapshoot for job seeker and employer alike. The main objective is to match a chef's passion with an owner's fiscal expectation… sounds simple, but it would be easier to carve a roast beef with a screwdriver. The result of these interviews is often a chemical reaction between projected food costs and creative impulses that inevitably leaves the chef bitter, enraged, and undoubtedly defeated. Home come the Birkenstocks, Henkel knives, and 100 pounds of culinary books, where they collect dust until their next tour of duty begins.

I had heard stories of the elite few, the culinary gods who made their mark in well-known restaurants and hotel kitchens with creations reminiscent of Iron Chef episodes, which was all I thought it took to guarantee a wonderful relationship between employer and employee. However, despite any love at first bite encounters I'd had they all ended badly, the once hoped for fruitful partnership between chef and owner in fact soured long before it ever had the chance to ripen. Because really, who among us can gaze into a crystal ball and make accurate predictions based on a few interviews and cooking demonstrations? A demonstration is really nothing more than a vague representation of a chef's expertise, accentuated by a few entrees, soup, a cold sandwich, and an appetizer or two. Should this be the basis for a monumental business decision, a culinary marriage between the love of food and the bottom line? Not! If you think the divorce rate is high in this country, try following the food section and classifieds in your particular area and your friggin head will spin. Whether it's a busy metropolis or a humble backwater town, a chef changes jobs more than Cher changes her look. So you can understand my skepticism about interviews, especially if they go well. Those good ones are the worst because the expectations are so high and in the end, you crash so hard. Jesus, I'm just a few pages into this catharsis and already I need a cigarette break (one of the many unhealthy byproducts of this highly stressful, relationship-damaging, and cholesterol-raising career). It is so funny how most of America perceives this profession as something glamorous and exciting, when in fact they couldn't be more wrong. Just ask my wife and kids, my aching back and fallen arches, my scarred arms and damaged liver and yellow teeth and low bank account.

Within walking distance from my house is a Tarot card reader. Seeking her predictions before interviews and accepting jobs has been a habit of mine for a couple of years. So with a few drags left on my cigarette I strolled over to her shop for a spiritual litmus test. I was shown into her inner sanctum and took a seat facing north to her south. My hope was for her to predict that I would finally find a job I could stick with, something that has never even slightly been reflected on my resume. The cards were laid in the more popular Celtic method (whatever that means, since neither of us was very Celtic). My past career experiences were shown aptly in the cards, symbolized with depictions of swords through the back, hearts tried by pain, and tragic falls from high towers. My fears, opinions, and hopes also were shown to hold true with cards of lovers, sacks of coins, and a big warm happy sun. Next came the main part of the reading, the card holding my fate, the card for what my money is really paying for. I looked down. Slowly the card was turned—the Queen of Cups, a depiction of royalty, and a woman of success, beauty, and power. This was normally a very positive sign, but in this case, she was upside down.

"Beware of the Queen of Cups," the Tarot card reader said.

Beware of the Queen of Cups, I thought. *What the hell does that mean?*

I wanted to believe in her powers, no matter how much I thought it was probably bullshit. The few times she predicted my future, she had kind of hit the mark. She told me that a restaurant I was going to buy with my wife would never work out and that another new restaurant I was opening would go bankrupt within a year. One other time she urged me not to accept a chef position from her fear of a card with a raging fire consuming a young man and his surroundings. I don't know if it meant anything, but unfortunately, the chef that did get hired burned the restaurant down. Ironically, it was named that year's hottest new restaurant in the city.

Couldn't I just once get a card with a chef wearing a happy face or something? No, not me, I only get the "beware of the Queen of Cups." From the way she warned me I expected the Mystery Machine to pull up beside me at any minute, with Scooby Doo, Shaggy, and the rest of the gang volunteering their services to solve the mystery of the queen of cups. Ah well, it would be all good as long as I got to be tied up with Daphne.

I left Madame Miriam and began my short walk home. All that remained before my interview was a warm bath, a couple of bedtime stories for my children, a goodnight kiss for my wife, and a restless night's sleep.

CHAPTER TWO

"Day after day, life turns gray like *the skin of a dying old man. Night after night, we pretend it's all-right…*" Pink Floyd's soothing melodies provided needed therapy as I drove to my impending interview. It was a bleak January day, with weather more appropriate for a funeral than an interview. I was driving down the highway to the unknown, and I realized there was just time and space separating me from my first job opportunity in the last 10 months. I couldn't believe it had been that long since my own restaurant debacle, in which, after months of hard work and all of my family's savings, my dreams of owning my own place were shot to shit in one foul swoop thanks to the con man we thought we were legitimately buying the restaurant from. Back then, I thought this whole working for other people crap was soon to be over, but by the looks of things, I couldn't have been more wrong.

This story began with an inconspicuous ad in the city paper. Usually I don't read the classifieds for employment opportunities; the majority of my matches have been made via the peers and associates I've stumbled across during my travels.

You must understand I learned my craft working in busy restaurants and plush hotels up and down the East coast. I've made long commutes to fine-dining suburban eateries, and I have supported many major city mass transit operations. I've had my share of Saturday nights in busy kitchens trying to keep up with the dupe express (the machine that prints out orders), while attempting to fend off every smart-mouthed waiter's sarcastic remarks and every waitress's screw-ups with a decorum that would make any culinary school alumni beam with honor. Needless to say, the attempts at keeping my cool weren't always successful.

So anyway, I answered an ad from the Sunday paper that went as follows:

> PRIVATE CHEF
> Great working conditions, good hours, experience in fine dining a must. 15 minutes from Center City, salary based on individual's skills. Call or fax to set up appointment

I'm surprised this ad caught my eye, because I never saw myself as private chef material. I always thought that this area of the business was for the ultra-fortunate or the poser dieticians/nutritionists who had the nerve to call themselves chefs. I am a talented chef, but don't take me for an egomaniac, I am also am a grunt, a cog, and sometimes even a ghost in the machine. I have no delusions of grandeur about this business, and a personal chef job was something I had thought to be unattainable.

Besides, being a chef is not all it's cracked up to be. I know (and certainly hear repeatedly from my parents and acquaintances) about all the potential perks. People have this idea that any chef can achieve TV stardom like my fellow alum Emeril has experienced, or that a chef can easily open their own successful restaurant, pen a best-selling cookbook, or receive a career-making rave review in a newspaper by an accomplished food critic. I'm a realist though; I've tried owning my own restaurant and gotten screwed. I've received fabulous write-ups in urban publications from picky food writers, only to get fired two weeks later. I have cooked for star-studded line-ups at esteemed benefit dinners, but the luster wears off pretty damn quick. It seems likely my entire career has been defined within a middle class salary bracket, complete with the all-inclusive sore back, callused hands, black lungs, coffee-stained teeth, and belly full of draft beer. So basically, what I'm saying is, don't believe the hype, it is all bullshit. For every Emeril there are a million disgruntled, underpaid, stressed out, and defeated chefs.

The interview was taking place in a posh hotel, one owned by the family that I was about to interview for, a hotel not unlike the ones I spent so many brutal years. To many people, a hotel is just a convenient stopover to rest your bones and tired eyes during long trips on the road, with an adjacent Shoney or Bob's Big Boy for your coffee fixes and patty melts.

But where I've worked is not the 30-room roach motel in the middle of bum fuck Iowa. I'm talking about million-dollar, five-star properties catering to the rich and famous, where full occupancy is equal to that of a small city. Here, restaurants are distinguished between fine dining and fine, *fine* dining. This is not exactly the kind of place that would offer unlimited soup and salads, we're talking a la carte territory. I wouldn't be surprised if each grind of the pepper mill over your Caesar salad at places like this didn't cost extra. These hotels leave chocolate mints on your 300-count Egyptian cotton pillowcase; they have mini bars full of macadamia nuts and tiny bottles of your favorite alcohol; places with concierges and maitre D's and a lot of other snobby-sounding French words.

However, deep inside these lavishly decorated architectural beauties lurks the closest thing to life before there were government regulations in the workplace, especially during the holidays. As soon as your time card gets punched, your seemingly endless 18-hour day is filled with chopping, peeling, straining, creating emulsions, breaking **emulsions**, fixing emulsions, finishing sauces, seasoning soups, cracking eggs, burning brûlées, infusing oils, blackening fish, **trussing** chickens, pin boning salmon, rendering fat, caramelizing onions, roasting garlic. Or you get to do the timeless classic—scraping gills out of frozen forty-pound blocks of lobster bodies for the preparation of lobster bisque (they leave tiny cuts along my fingers that say hello whenever I squeeze lemon into the Chardonnay **beurre blance** or fresh lime juice into the mango papaya salsa).

So yeah, to be a professional chef, whether you're in a hotel or restaurant setting, is pure heaven on earth, but unfortunately it springs from the bowels of hell. God, how I hate the Food Network for putting grandiose ideas in people's heads!

Where was I? Oh yeah, the interview. Arriving at the hotel and all that. I parked my car a good walking distance from the entrance so that the odor of my Marlboro cigarette would have ample time to wear off. My attire was a notch above casual; I didn't want to make too good of an impression, and one I couldn't live up to in the future. Besides, I dressed more like Field and Stream than GQ on a normal day. When I arrived, I immediately went to the restroom and splashed some water on my cleanly shaven face, then ventured out to find the right door.

I sat for a few minutes in a waiting room reading, of all things, People Magazine, until a middle-aged chef called me into a nicely decorated office. A small session of mind-numbing small talk took place for a while before any real cards were laid on the table. Besides comparing personal horror stories, we touched upon some of our more youthfully naive experiences in the biz, each one trying to raise the ladder a peg. I do think I bested him with my tale of the time I made two full steam kettles of smoked lobster **consommé** with an essence of **lemongrass** and a garnish of mini lobster raviolis for a Robert Mondovi dinner featuring guest chefs such as Wolfgang Puck, Gunther Seeger, and Troy Thompson (A-list celebrities in the restaurant world).

My interviewer scanned my resume and asked me the same, although appropriate, questions I'd heard many times before. Why did I leave there? What did you learn here? How long did you work there? And so on and so on. He was a good interviewer and the perfect person to do it since he was currently the personal chef that I would possibly replace. As the interview progressed, I grew more confident. I figured I had it made since he would tell me all the small things about a job that make it what it is that can't be conveyed by an outsider. We continued to chat while he casually brushed over salary, health benefits, and working conditions. I figured he would wait until they chose a chef before giving any real details.

Finally, he asked how I felt about doing a cooking demonstration at the house of the prospective employers that very evening. The way he said it led me to believe that it was not an option. He went on to say that they already had two other applicants cook for them and that they wanted to make their decision as soon as possible. So, realizing I didn't have much of a choice, I agreed. As I saw it, if I could ace this cooking demonstration I would be in. I assumed the other two candidates didn't knock the rich couples' monogrammed socks off or else this guy wouldn't be interviewing me.

Besides, cooking for prospective employers was a normal procedure at this point in my career, although it was usually done at a restaurant or some sort of professional kitchen. It's common in this industry because you can only delve so far into a person's soul through the elegant font and neat punctuation of a well-crafted resume. Cooking is a passion, not a piece of colored stationary, so you sometimes have to prove you can do what your resume says you can do.

My ego was large enough at that time to feel confident enough to show them my stuff and do a great job. So I followed the chef to the private residence high in the hills above the city, but first we made a short detour to the grocery store. The chef told me that the lady of the house had called him on his cell phone with dinner requests, mainly concerning the entrée. Her request was lobster, preferably grilled. I went over some menu options in my head as I ventured down the supermarket aisles. I decided to just pick the freshest ingredients I could find and basically let my creativity and the clock take over.

With our brief shopping expedition completed, it was back in my car for another round of "follow the leader." The chef said he wanted to show me a shortcut. I kept noticing his bullshit grin and chuckles under his breath. I was beginning to not like this guy; his attitude was definitely starting to rub me the wrong way. The good interviewer he started out to be vanished. He was starting to make me feel uneasy. I felt as if he was Captain Hook walking me down a plank. In a perfect world there would be solidarity among us chefs, brethren linked by creativity and a burning zeal to cook, and cook well. A good chef cooking great food is no different from a poet writing passionate prose. We rely on the same emotion that musicians use for weaving scattered melodies into inspired ballads. The sweat and tears an artist endures to create their masterpiece, chefs share in the sweaty basements of city establishments. So why does this guy seem like such a big prick? We should be fellow seamen in the turbulent seas of sleepless nights, third-degree burns, and stitch-needing gashes that are tended to with duck tape. We are both destined to travel from place to place repeatedly trying to earn uneasily given respect from insolent waiters and vapid waitresses, delinquent dishwashers, numerous cooks, and the integral regular clientele. Maybe he had limited social skills, or maybe I was just being insecure. But it wasn't my imagination; he was being a cocky son of a bitch, that was for certain. But that's not so unusual. Cockiness is a popular characteristic among us Jonahs languishing in the stomach of this whale of a food service industry. I just couldn't put a finger on it but I really think something was not all that it seemed with him. Maybe it was just this feeling of dishonesty he was putting out.

As we drove through the streets, my thoughts on him vanished and were replaced with sights of mighty oaks, elms, and maples that filled the landscapes and studded the neighborhood we were driving through. I was in awe of flowing bushes and shrubs exotically designed and meticulously kept. Gothic statues and marble figurines adorned magnificent properties, these present-day gardens of Eden where the only thing missing were naked people slightly covered with fig leaves running around the place. Iron gates, endless driveways, and roads so smoothly paved I barely had to press on my gas pedal greeted me as we glided along the twisty, turny roads of rural Main Line suburbia. Each house we passed was larger then the next. Some estates were actually titled, given names as if they were living entities.

When the chef's turn signal finally blinked, we were in the process of passing a property that had enough land to house a third-world country. I saw rolling hills, majestic trees, endless gardens, man-made ponds with arcing bridges, all neatly enclosed in black iron gating reminiscent of Fort Knox. The overall appearance of the house itself struck me as odd. It had a historic 1800s sense of craftsmanship paired with 20th-century modernization. A state of the art addition to a stately manor…Gee, why didn't I think of that? Maybe because I'm just so happy in my three-bedroom, one-bathroom apartment oasis? Or maybe because I'm missing a few dozen 0's at the end of my bank account balance?

I followed the chef down another small driveway into a parking area (more like a "parking lot"). The perimeter had a series of single garages, 10 in all, and one 6-door garage. I parked my ratty Nissan Sentra, with all its coffee stains, cigarette burns, and aroma of stale garlic and onions. It looked pretty out of place among the collection of automobiles, which included three shiny new SUVs, a Moby Dick white Mercedes, a brilliant red Lamborghini, a jet black Maserati, and another Mercedes of some shade of blue. This was the "servants entrance," I was told, and servants were only permitted to enter this way, not through the 24-hour surveillanced, "King Kong"-sized gated entrance that led to a cobblestone path for family members, their closest friends, and the rest of their "caviar crowd" and filthy rich acquaintances.

My arms were feeling heavy from carrying the grocery bags through the "property" towards the "servant's house entrance". The chef conveniently carried nothing except an attitude that became gruffer and more aloof the closer we got to the kitchen. He made no comments about the pagoda-like garden, 12-foot high water fall, and marble benches we strolled by. He offered me no anecdotes about the studio filled with paintings and pastel drawings that sat adjacent to the main house. He gave no insight into the cabana that stood next to an Olympic-sized swimming pool around which sat more elegant lounge chairs than most swim clubs. He just silently walked a couple paces ahead of me, leading me past the large trash house, onto a smaller path and then under a roofed porch.

On the porch was a large gas grill, which caused him finally to utter something. "You've never seen a grill like this one," he said at me, not really to me. A couple of potted plants and a lounge chair made up the rest of the porch's décor, and I couldn't help but admire it. This place was right out of a glossy magazine. At least he opened the screen door for me, and I stepped into a foyer or mudroom, I'm not sure what they're called in mansions. I tried to get a quick look around but was interrupted by two huge white sheepdogs by the names of Anthony and Cleopatra. The slimmer and more graceful of the two wore white ribbons in her hair and smelled of perfume. The pompous, more rotund one had a thick solid gold collar around his thick neck. The dogs gave me a quick once over with a few sniffs and smells, but then turned their attention toward the other chef, showing him much more affection. It was an uncomfortable display; I'd rather not go into detail, although I will tell you that tongues seemed to touch. After this questionable display of man-dog affection, I was swiftly led into a laundry room. It housed your average high-end washer and dryer as well as a two-bay slop sink along one wall. A few hooks holding chef jackets, butler uniforms, and maid outfits made up another wall. On the longest wall was a refrigerator/freezer and cases of imported beers, sodas, and bottled waters stacked to the ceiling, I felt like I was in a bomb shelter. The chef's first words to me since we entered the house were mere instructions.

"Change into a chef coat and meet me in the kitchen," he said before he went to announce our arrival.

Great. If I wasn't nervous before I sure was now. I felt as if I had fallen into a story from the "Twilight Zone" where I ended up in some bizarre parallel universe. I was usually more self-assured and confident in pressure situations, but my shaking hands turned the buttoning of my chef jacket into a complicated challenge.

"I need to relax, take a deep breath or two," I said aloud. "I'm just going to cook a little bit, that's all, it's just cooking, or is it? Who did I need to impress? I'm a great chef no matter what happens. I am... right?"

Suddenly I realized the absurdity of talking to myself in the laundry room of a mansion, but I couldn't stop. "I know I can do this. I CAN do this, I can do this, and I'm just going to cook, clean up, and go.... That's all."

I was beginning to annoy myself.

"This isn't rocket science!" I yelled at myself. "I'm not fucking curing cancer, I can do this. Take a deep breath... Relax." I was beginning to hyperventilate. "FUCK ... I can't do this!"

"Wait, I CAN do this, but I don't want to do this, yeah that's it." My hands were going numb. "Wait, this is crazy, I'm going crazy. I'll just leave, I'll sneak out."

I was formulating a plan in my panic-stricken mind. *That's what I'll do. I'm out of here. He'll call me tomorrow and I'll just say I wasn't the right person for the job ... no big deal.*

"Brian!" I heard the chef call.

"Aaaaah, oh yeah, yeah, I'm coming, yeah, here I come!" I answered rather overzealously.

Shit…shit, shit, shit, I chanted under my breath.

"Yeah, here I come," I yelled as I softly continued my chant even softer. *Fuck, fuck, fuck.*

I swallowed my pride, scooped up the grocery bags, and went to meet the chef in the kitchen a mere 15 reluctant steps away. The ground rules were set right away.

"It's 4:00 p.m. now and dinner is at 7:00 p.m.," he informed me. "You need to prepare an appetizer, entrée—preferably grilled lobster—and a dessert for two people. Josie will show you what plates to use." He motioned toward an elderly woman in a maid's outfit. "She will also serve the food. The regular butler needed off today."

Oh the horrors, you just can't find good help these days, I thought sarcastically to myself.

He turned to leave with no wishes of good luck or words of encouragement. I was speechless; I just stood there with my mouth agape. Then he suddenly stopped and turned toward me.

I thought, *Thank god, some last-second advice.*

Uh, no, I was wrong. He only curtly mentioned, "I'll call you if it goes well. If not, I won't bother you." And off he went.

There I was, standing alone in someone's house that I haven't even met and these mystery people expected dinner in roughly three short hours. I hadn't a clue to their tastes, no familiarity with their kitchen, and I hadn't even ironed out a menu for Christ's sake. I was pacing around a large rectangle Corrian counter top, double stainless steel sink, and butcher-block island. Custom cherry wood cabinets with crystal-clear glass doors, shelves of expensive cookbooks, and more Corrian topped counters equipped with all sorts of kitchen appliances and culinary gadgets ran along the outsides of the two long walls. My pacing continued past the twin Sub Zero refrigerator/freezer, the Vulcan 6 burner range with broiler and industrial hood and ventilation system, and into what I would deem as their pantry, one that happened to be bigger then most people's entire kitchens. It contained every flavored oil, vinegar, canned good, spice, sugar, and flour imaginable, along with pans, pots, sheet pans, and just about every gadget that could be found in your average culinary store. Finally, I stopped pacing; I thought I had better pull myself together instead of pulling my pud. I needed to finalize this menu! All I needed was one three-course menu, that was all, and I had literally thousands of options to choose from. One three-course menu… for all the marbles.

And the menu was….

CHAPTER THREE

THE FIRST COURSE WOULD BE CRUCIAL. I had to let them know that I meant business. The reality was, this course would act as a food version of a hello and a handshake. It needed to be powerful in flavor as well as in presentation, an edible representation of my style and ability. I would be expressing my passion and love for cooking, showing proper respect for each ingredient, providing an acknowledgement on the importance of using the freshest bounties of the seasons, and above all, showing no fear. The best chef I'd ever worked for always said, "The food will sense your fear and the flavors will hide. Never show fear." I have never forgotten this credo and, as I've aged, it continues to make more and more sense.

First Course
Roasted Beet Napoleon

Beautiful red and golden yellow beets are slowly roasted at 325 degrees. They glisten from a thin coat of olive oil and are perched on a bed of kosher salt. They sit king and queen filled to the brim with essential vitamins and minerals, becoming sweeter and sweeter with each passing moment. Their natural sugars and flavors are being enhanced by time and heat. An occasional addition of white wine to the roasting pan remedies dry and cracked skin. In just one short hour, root vegetables, as hard as rocks, transform into the mildly textured and bold flavored beauties they were meant to be. After cooling, a sharp paring knife peels away the shriveled skin. The rich colored orbs stand naked on the cutting board, ready to be sliced into 1/4-inch rounds. Each slice will be seasoned with a touch of kosher salt and fresh ground white pepper before being used in the final presentation.

To create the "Napoleon" (a layering of various ingredients in a stacklike formation), I chose mild, slightly soft goat cheese. Some goat's cheese tends to be a bit strong, but this one possessed just the right tang. Accompanying the beets and goat cheese are Anjou pears, crisp and delicately sweet, a perfect accompaniment to round out the other flavors. One slice of red beet, two slivers of pear, a dollop of goat cheese, one slice of yellow beet, two slivers of pear, a dollop of goat cheese, and up the stack grew. I gently place the multi-colored tower in the middle of a 9-inch China plate. On top of the tower, I placed a tiny potion of mache (small, tender, and buttery leaf greens, also known as lamb's lettuce) tossed gingerly with hazel nut oil, French imported champagne vinegar, and fresh snipped chives. Seconds before the plates were to be served, I drizzled lightly heated hazelnut vinaigrette around the plate. An intoxicating aroma filled the air; I quickly placed coarse chopped toasted hazelnuts and a few shafts of chive, cut on the bias, as final garnish. The maid picked up the plates and walked out towards the dining room. Dinner had officially begun.

Going on the assumption that I had sufficiently wetted their appetites, the stage was now set for Act II, the true culinary climax of the evening. You see, a good meal is not unlike a well-written book. It cannot hold its weight with merely a strong beginning or finale. It must be strong throughout, substantial throughout, good from start to finish. Just one error, one careless flaw, and both the book and the meal become just ordinary.

This course, unlike the others, was requested. At least in its main element—lobster, preferably grilled. The grilling of lobster, however, has never been my favorite method of preparation, but what the hell. "Carpe Diem!" I told myself I was the Grill Master, master of the grill and all outdoor open fires. Able to char, blacken, sear, and scorch even the mightiest of BBQ fares. Besides, especially in this business, the customer is always right. I gave the people what they wanted.

Main Course
Grilled Lobster - Celery Root Risotto - Broiled Asparagus

Long ago, many moons before I was born, a creature of strange appearance surfaced from the watery depths, with oversized claws and bumpy skeletal exterior, its only way to protect their dreamy, luscious flesh. Ever since then, these marine marvels have graced menus. Their plump claws and meaty tails have been considered delicacies to the highbrows, the lowbrows, and all brows in between.

I chose two female three pounders, the female lobsters being the more tender and tastier gender. The challenge in cooking lobster, no matter what method used, is making sure the claws and tails are not overcooked. No one wants to pay $15 to $20 dollars a pound to dip pieces of rubber into drawn butter and lemon.

First, I combined unsalted butter with some basil, parsley, paprika, fresh lemon juice, salt, and pepper in a food processor, blending until smooth. With a sharp **French knife** I now became executioner, driving the tip of the blade into the upper spine area below the heads of our two ladies. It's a cooking science theory that if a lobster is released from its life in this manner, opposed to murder through boiling water, the flesh will be more tender. The sudden kill of being dropped into a cauldron of scalding water causes the lobster to constrict its muscles, thus causing a tougher product. Besides, it's a mitzvah to be compassionate towards every living thing. (Lobster, by the way, is not kosher, but most people overlook that footnote from the good book.) The lobsters are then split from head to tail, making sure to cut just through the meat and to leave the shell connected. The lobsters lay spread eagle on the table as I dismembered the claws from the body and cracked them slightly with the back of the knife. I put the claws on the grill first, covered with a pie pan, 6 to 8 minutes per side. The lobster bodies are then brushed with olive oil and seasoned. Flesh side down, they are dropped onto the red-hot grates. Sublime smells mingled with the crisp evening air, and over medium high heat for 10 minutes the lobster meat got a nice char on the outside and the shell turned a vibrant deep red. The cooked lobsters are slathered with the seasoned butter and are ready to be plated.

The celery root "risotto" is a specialty of mine. I take the winter vegetable and breathe vitality and spirit into its dull existence. At first glance the root may leave you repulsed because of its knotty, dirty, brown skin. However, underneath its rough-looking exterior is an extremely versatile milky, white flesh, which in this case, I dice into a medium **brunoise.** A sweating of minced onion and shallot in a heavy pan begins the process; the slow cooking of these guys in some butter and olive oil until tender and translucent will provide foundation and depth to the risotto. Adding the celery root is next. With a wooden spoon I stir the morsels into the sweetened onion bath and season with salt and pepper. Meticulously, I move the ingredients round and round the pot, the first sign of tenderness in the celery root, no less exhilarating than the first sign of spring. Next I drop a fresh laurel leaf (bay leaf) into the pot. An addition of white wine reduces into the porous vegetables. This is immediately followed by just enough chicken stock to cover the "risotto." Risotto traditionally is an Italian dish made with Arborio rice, and always denotes a dish made with much stirring, love, and attention. Whereas the risotto is laboriously stirred over low heat, allowing the liquid to ever so slowly be absorbed, the celery root simmers until it is softened, but not mushy. I finish the risotto with a spoon of whipped heavy cream, a chunk of whole butter, fresh thyme, and chopped chives. I check for seasoning and my taste buds give their solemn approval.

The asparagus I kept simple, using a preparation I've grown fond of over the years. I start with firm-tipped, medium stalks. I lop off the woody discolored portion from the bottoms, and then gently peel the first layer of skin for better texture and appearance. Lightly oiled and seasoned, the asparagus is lined up in a dish like soldiers atop 1-inch thick lemon round slices that also are oiled and seasoned. Into a very hot oven they go and roast for 6 to 8 minutes. Right before they are pulled from the heated chamber, they are flashed under the fiery broiler. The asparagus should still be **al dente** (firm to the bite). The roasted lemon rounds are released of their juices over the awaiting spears to complete the dish.

The maid served the grilled lobster, risotto, and asparagus on a large silver platter. From the looks of the emptied platter she brought back into the kitchen I concluded the second course was a success.

To compare a chef to a pastry chef is like comparing dogs to cats or night to day—the whole mindset between the two is vastly different. In both preparation and procedure, the process of baking the sweet confections everybody loves is more along the lines of a scientific experiment than the artistic flair of cooking. Exact amounts must be used; even a tiny measurement over or under the recipe's directions could create unfixable problems for the finished product. On top of this reality, the aspect of time becomes an obstacle; one doesn't just whip up a cake or homemade ice cream. Pie dough or meringue shells don't miraculously appear to be filled and served. Frozen berries don't turn into tasty **coulis** with hardly a thought. In most cases, a pastry chef has the basic components of a plated dessert at his or her disposal, and then builds upon that to create a finished masterpiece. My own thin experience in the pastry arts wasn't helping much either. Except for a few classes in college many years ago and my designing of dessert menus in previous chef positions, I've dabbled very little on that side of the kitchen. With all this being taken into consideration, I chose a basic but flavorful dessert that puts an intriguing twist on a popular fruit.

Dessert Course
Strawberry and Sambuca Flambé over French Vanilla Ice Cream

Plump sweet strawberries from California are stemmed, quartered, and piled high in a glass **ramekin**. In a sauté pan over medium heat, whole butter and the white crystals of cane sugar merge to create a bubbly froth of tasty goodness. As it heats, the sugary, viscous, liquid melts to autumn amber. The ramekin of strawberries is tipped into the pan. It's as sublime a moment as you or I slipping into a hot bubble bath. I coat each portion of the cratered fruit in the hot sweetness before pulling the pan away from the flame. I add Sambuca and strawberry liquor and POOF, a burst of jagged flames arise as the pan goes back over the fire (hence the term **flambé**). The alcohol in the liquor ignites and burns off, and only the flavors of hot strawberry and anise remain in the shiny red juices. A few turns of a peppermill accent the dish, thus providing an unusual but tasty twist.

A few healthy spoonfuls are cascaded over three medium scoops of ice cream. A sprig of fresh mint in the middle of this luscious triangle completes the presentation.

CHAPTER FOUR

After cleaning the kitchen, the maid who served the dinner approached me and in broken English told me I could go.

"What about meeting them?" I asked, pointing toward the door to the dining room. I had a sinking feeling that they didn't want or expect to meet me.

"Yous can go," she said, as politely and unemotional as the first time. "I'll take that from ya." She must have been referring to the chef jacket I put on earlier in the laundry room. As she put out her callused hand, I handed her the dirty jacket as if she were my maid too.

To her, the coat was just a piece of house property and naturally must stay. That Miss Josie was a funny old bird. She had to be at least 75, and with her native Mexican tongue she spoke Spanish much more fluently than her adopted English. I never once got any indication from her about how I was doing the whole night. The only time she showed any type of emotion was when she ate her dinner; she wanted no part of any of my concoctions. Instead, she cracked open a tin of King Oscar sardines, doused them with some kind of **Oxacaan** hot sauce, slapped them between two pieces of white bread, and chowed down. A diet coke and a sugar cookie for dessert completed her quaint dinner.

I took Miss Josie's advice and called it a night. I walked outside and immediately felt an overwhelming feeling of exhilaration engulf me. I emphatically pumped my fist hard into the dark and chilly air. I felt that no matter what their opinions were, I knew down deep that I kicked ass.

I lit up a cigarette and took a long drag. I was free for the moment, free to enjoy my self-proclaimed victory as I puffed my way back to my car and tried to navigate my way out the mansion maze. I arrived home 2 hours later not quite sure how I found my way out, with my feeling of accomplishment dimmed somewhat.

CHAPTER FIVE

Morning arrived, and like any other unemployed dad who happened to be a chef, I took orders for breakfast. I knew that I could at least cook for my two boys, who were home because of winter break. Naturally, they both wanted chocolate-chip pancakes. Good choice, I thought. Pancakes are one of the few recipes my kids will actively help making; It must be a batter thing. Kids in general seem to have strong tendencies to being the one who gets to lick the spoon, spatula, or whip. No matter the implement, the leftover batter from any cake, brownie, or cookie leaves kids drooling. Usually pancake batter doesn't fall into the same category as the other much sweeter mixtures, but the addition of chocolate chips more than did the trick. Together we added the ingredients to the stainless steel bowl, their sleepy eyes perking up with each stolen chocolate morsel entering their blood stream.

"Dad?" my older son asked. "Did your dad make chocolate chip pancakes for you, when you were a boy?"

"No, no, Pop Pop didn't really do much cooking, he was more of a go out to eat guy." I explained. "He liked to take us out for breakfast or dinner, not cook it."

"Oh, so you cook for us because you're real good at it, or something like that?" he went on, smiling like an angel, awaiting my answer.

"Is that true, Dad?" my younger boy asked, not wanting to be left out of the conversation.

"It's something like that," I replied as Brooks, my oldest, cracked the eggs and added the oil.

Daniel, my 6 year old, added the flour and milk, and they both took turns mixing until most of the lumps were gone. My boys are my pride and joy, and because of them, I am happy my restaurant deal fell through. I took it as a sign from above. Hell, with 80% of all restaurants failing within their first year, who needed to take that kind of financial risk? The 7-day workweeks would have never let me see my kids. Just being a chef for others kept me away from birthday parties, little league games, holiday gatherings, and Memorial Day BBQs. What did I think? Working for myself would be different? I therefore concluded that it must have been a sign from above.

Being unemployed for 10 months was not a case of laziness. I needed some quality time to get to know my children again, not to mention my wife. Basically, I needed time to decompress and rekindle the family's flame.

"It's about time," I said aloud. I didn't think I could wait much longer.

Beth was finally up. I could hear her stirring upstairs by the sounds of her little feet treading above on the hardwood floors. Last night when I came home all I wanted to do was tell her about my day but she was sleeping so soundly. I told myself it could wait. Besides, I didn't want to act like I wanted the job…or perhaps needed the job so badly. My wife is an endless fountain of patience. She has put up with so much of my bullshit, coming home drunk at all hours of the morning, too tired to ever help around the house on my infrequent days off.

"Oh, I could go on," I muttered. "But those days are over."

"What days are over?" she asked sleepily, overhearing my mumbling. I acted like I didn't hear her.

It was she who brought the classified ad to my attention. She knew our relationship couldn't handle another traditional position in this business. So it was no surprise when she asked how it went while biting her lip, her emotions reflecting a roller coaster ride on her face.

"What happened?" she repeated, her eyes filling with hope. "What did you have to do?"

How *did* it go? I thought to myself. I wanted to answer the question just right, but a lot of things about the experience were still, although fresh, convoluted in my head. After a lengthy pause, I told her about the verbal interview at the hotel. I told her about the dick-head chef, the menu, and the house.

"WHAT?" she yelled, interrupting me mid-sentence. "You didn't even meet them? What does that mean? They didn't even come into the kitchen?" Her voice was angry with disbelief.

I rolled my eyes and shrugged my shoulders. "Maybe they are eccentric or something. All I know is that I cooked a good meal, and I think everything went great. The chef will call if they want me."

"More pancakes!" the children roared form the kitchen table. That ended the conversation, just as the phone rang.

It must have been serendipity. My caller ID was showing that the telephone call was from the chef. *O.K. here we go,* I thought to myself.

"Hello?" I said, trying to sound unassuming.

The chef said, "You're hired. They loved the meal, and they have agreed to your salary request."

Damn, I knew I should have asked for more money! After a couple of minutes of unmemorable banter I accepted the offer, hung up the phone, and turned to see my wife smiling from ear to ear.

"Well honey, unemployment is officially over," I said.

CHAPTER SIX

I WAS ANXIOUSLY AWAITING THE START OF MY new job. I usually considered my workday to begin the minute my head comes off the pillow. If I can't lounge around the house in my loose sweats, right hand anchored to a mug of coffee, while the other turns the sports page, then for this day I am in fact somebody else's property. Freedom is a state of elation with no constraints or shackles; workdays are filled to the brim with nothing but constraints and shackles. It isn't until the puppet master cuts his strings that I consider my workday to be over. I suppose I have another thirty-five some odd years of being a human puppet, being paid to perform for the amusement of others.

It was my first day at the new job. Sure, I was aware of the countless people who spend years and years at the same job mucking and grinding their way to pensions and plaques outlining their years of service. I seem destined to not be one of those people. A first day of a new job may not occur for me every day, but experiencing one every 6 months to a year wouldn't be a stretching it. My combustible personality could have something to do with it, but this trait is not all that uncommon for chefs. Most chefs are known to throw a pot or two, so chefs play the game of musical restaurants, one going here, one going there, and around and round they go.

This first day had a slightly different feel to it. I was anxious, like the start of any other job, but I was also mightily curious. Curious to learn what life is really like behind the doors of the rich and famous. How do they live? Is it like the movies or television? What was it like to have all their money, cars, big houses, and things I don't know to question? How often have I wondered what my life would be like if I hit the powerball number? Well, these people have power balls coming out of their asses.

I couldn't shake the bizarre feeling of going to work in someone's house. This was not a restaurant, a hotel, or a banquet facility; I was actually going to work inside someone's house. I was to be their personal chef. My job was basically to cook any damn thing they want—to satisfy any craving their appetites might have. I was their employee, but was I also their servant? That was possibly my biggest fear. A personal chef I thought I could deal with, but a servant? I understand there was a fine line between being a servant and an employee, but a line existed nonetheless, one I refused to cross or be pushed over. That line was more than merely a symbolic divider; it was my manhood, my dignity, and my self-esteem, and I preferred to keep what little of those I had left after fifteen years in this fucking business.

Friday, January 19, was my official starting date. Winter was in full force, and a threat of snow had been forecasted for that evening. The sun gave off no warmth, yet it still shined its glaring beams through my windshield, reeking havoc on my ability to read the directions. I had only been to the house once while following the chef, and it was very dark when I left that night. I navigated through the remains of the morning rush hour traffic on the highway easily enough, but those unfamiliar side roads required all my attention. My starting time was 10:00 a.m. and the clock read 9:53 a.m. as I pulled into their driveway/parking lot.

I put a fresh chef jacket over my slightly worn semi-white T-shirt. I wore my own black and white check pants, along with trendy black **Birkenstocks.** I walked into the kitchen and noticed that unlike the day before it was much more crowded. The staff, a motley crew indeed, huddled themselves around the butcher-block island with the day's paper strewn across the table. They were all stuffing themselves with some sort of pastry or continental breakfast fare.

"Good morning, my name is Brian," I said, introducing myself as the new chef and fellow crewmember.

"Here, this is yours," a woman said, as a torn piece of white paper with writing on it was slid in my general direction. She was young, probably in her early thirties, clad in a tight-fitting black and white maid's outfit. She had curly brown hair, brown eyes, and some nice God-given features. She was cute, I guess, but with an unfriendly attitude like that…well, she's wasn't that cute.

Here, this is yours, she said to me, like I was working for *her*. No please or thank you or even a mild flirtation. Who the hell did she think she was? Even better, who the hell did she think I was? I was the chef, thank you! I got your right here…right here I thought.

Instead I said pleasantly, "And what is your name, sweetness?"

"I'm not your sweetness," she snapped. "My name is Michelle, thank you."

"Oh, it must be my pleasure." Sarcasm was creeping into my tone, so I decided to go with it. I extended my hand to the queen of clean, then pulled it back.

"I'm sorry, I better not, I haven't properly sterilized my hand," I drawled. "I wouldn't want to touch royalty with my unworthiness."

"Grrrr," she uttered and left the room, leaving behind her half-eaten bagel and juice glass.

Well, I'm off to a good start, I thought.

Josie just sat there in front of her tea and toast, not adding anything to the conversation.

"Well, my name is Francis," said the only other male in the room. "I am the property supervisor."

"You're the butler," Michelle laughed, entering back into the room just in time to correct him. "Property supervisor, my ass."

"Don't listen to her, she's a bitch," he continued. "If you is smart, you'll listen to me. I'm in charge, and she don't like it."

I could tell I wasn't dealing with a genius there, so I humored him with a nod.

"Helloooo!" A drawn-out and commanding voice sounded from an unknown source. The morning squabble ending quickly as everyone's attention quickly turned to the female voice on the machine. It felt like a weird Charlie's Angels scenario.

"Hello! Francis, Michelle, is anyone there?" Her second greeting was louder than the first.

"Hello, Mrs. B," Francis said.

"Am I on speaker?" the voice asked.

"No," said Francis as he quickly picked up the receiver and pressed a button on the phone. "Yes, okay, yes, yes, I'll tell him."

He hung up the phone and pulled a set of car keys out from his black jacket pocket.

"Lunch will be at 12:30, and Mr. will be coming home," he casually mentioned as he went out the door of the kitchen.

That must have also been the cue for the maids to leave as well. Josie went through the same door as the butler and Michelle went the other way. I was alone in the kitchen, but not entirely, as their mess was still there to keep me company. Since it was my first day I cleaned it up, but that wouldn't go on for much longer, I told myself. No way was I going to keep cleaning up after those frigging people. Anyway, I had more important things to deal with, like lunch at 12:30.

Lunch
Shrimp Nicoise

The way Francis said that Mr. B would be coming home for lunch made it sound as if it were an unusual occurrence. I figured maybe he was coming home since it was my first day. I decided to go with a classic Nicoise salad, but use shrimp as a substitute for the more traditional tuna. Six U-12 shrimp thawed while I prepped the other ingredients.

1. **Yukon gold potatoes.** Cut into small wedges and drop into boiling

salted water. Cook until tender and let cool at room temperature. Never run water over potatoes to cool them off (that will make them mushy). I learned the hard way from an insane chef at school. He was quite perturbed when I ruined 20 pounds of possible potato salad.

2. **Haricot Vert**. French green beans are plunged into boiling salted water. This is called **blanching**. It not only cooks the vegetable but also intensifies the color. After blanching, the beans are shocked. Shocking the hot items into ice cold water stops the cooking process immediately. Done right, the vegetables are cooked but still firm, their brilliant color and vitamins intact.

3. Grape tomatoes (a few red ones and a few yellow ones). These guys are sweet and delicious. I cut them in halves with a serrated knife, so not to hurt their delicate nature.

4. **Calamata olives**, juicy and slightly pungent. I extract just the flesh of these Greek fruits by slicing with a sharp paring knife down the contour of their pit. That way I get four slivers from each olive.

5. Artichokes, spiny globes form California. I cut off the inedible tops and cut off the outer skin. What is left after the cleaning is known as the artichoke heart. It will oxidize rather quickly, so I let the cleaned ones sit in a pool of lemon water. I quarter these hearts and proceed to **braise** them. What you do is sauté some slivers of fresh garlic in olive oil. Then add red pepper flakes and some fresh basil. Stir a bit, and then add the hearts, season with salt and fresh ground pepper. Sauté briefly and then deglaze with white wine. While the wine is evaporating, toss a bay leaf and a chunk of lemon to the pot. Pour some chicken stock about 1/3 up on the chokes. Cover the pot and let simmer for about 20 minutes. The chokes should suck up most of the liquid. Then you reseason and toss in a few drops of extra virgin olive oil. These guys are delicious all by themselves, but in this salad they really add an element of sophistication.

6. **Capers**, unopened flower buds, native to the Mediterranean region. I prefer the large, plump, fresh ones, the unjarred variety that are salt-cured and still intact with a stem. They have a sharp salty, sour flavor. I rinse and cut them into little round slices and use them sparingly in the salad.
7. Mixed greens, usually a combination of assorted lettuces like **radicchio, frissce, red and green oak, lola rosa**, and a few others. I also use snow peas shoots for extra texture, and some of the **mache** from last night.
8. Dressing, vinaigrette, made entirely using a blender. A few anchovy filets, a couple of caper berries, the juice of one fresh lemon, a tablespoon of Dijon mustard, an ounce of balsamic vinegar, and about 3 ounces of olive oil. Salt and pepper to taste. Puree it up and it's done.
9. Shrimp. Ones this big are usually called prawns. I simply peel and devein them. Save the shells for other uses in the freezer; remind me later to tell you what to do with them. Marinate the shrimp in some of the dressing. Drop their tasty bodies into a hot pan (no oil is needed because of the dressing). Sear on both sides, deglaze with white wine, and if need be, finish briefly in the oven. I just put the whole pan in for a couple minutes. You have to be careful because, like lobster, they will become rubber chew toys if cooked too long.
10. The salad construction goes like this. Mix all ingredients together, except the shrimp, with enough dressing just to coat everything, along with some chopped scallion or chive. Consider this fact: Too much dressing is just as bad as not enough dressing, so don't go crazy. The extra will keep in the refrigerator for later uses. Pile the salad high in the center of a plate. Remember presentation is important. Keep it tight and together. If a **Chinese mandolin** is handy, like it is for me, run a peeled carrot through it. You will get vermicelli-like carrot threads that can be gathered into a tight,

bright orange ball for garnish on top of the salad. Put the sautéed shrimp around the salad. I put three on each plate at equal distance apart, and one on the top of the carrots. Voila. That was my shrimp Nicoise.

CHAPTER SEVEN

I ALLOWED MYSELF A MOMENT TO REFLECT ON the first afternoon of my new job. Lunch went well, the meal was tasty and well presented, but other than that, there was nothing too positive to report. Am I ever going to meet these people, I wondered? I had now cooked two meals in their kitchen and yet could not pick either of them out of a lineup. Who I could pick out was the bleached blonde, 100-pound pussy that titled himself property manager. I guessed that all rich and pretentious families were obligated to have one of those fellows around. His position should really have been titled Chief Ass-Kisser. He was the liaison between the family and the rest of us lowly commoners. He was the one who provided me with the shopping money, served the food, acted as chauffeur, communicated with the gardeners, and answered the phone, door, or anything else that rang. He was the boss in our caste pecking order. Then we had the goddess of grime, the chief toilet washer and underwear folder of the second floor. She seemed to be a real delight. Obviously, I would have to deal with both of them if I was going to last there for any amount of time. Finally, we had Josie; she was the live-in maid, who was responsible for the first floor, and let's just say her best years were behind her. With her questionable legal status, limited education, and Stepford-like devotion to the family, she had been with Mr. B for 42 years and practically raised their youngest son.

While reading over the list Michelle gave me first thing that morning, I could see that food items weren't the only things this personal chef was responsible to purchase. That was just the start of a growing list of odd duties the previous chef conveniently forgot to tell me about during my interview. I was a little puzzled by the quantities of these items; the amounts seemed outrageous to me. They seemed even more so when I found out that what she gave me was only a partial list of essentials that the house must have in stock at all times.

Chef–
I need today -
Ivory Soap Detergent 12 bottles LARGE ONLY
Niagara Starch 8 cans MUST BE BLUE CAN
Toilet tissue, 4 12-packs
Lysol Liquid Cleanser 14 bottles ANY SCENT BUT LEMON
Dove Soap Bars 24 bars
Diet Coke 6 cases ONLY CANS
Sprite 6 cases ONLY CANS
Bottled water 18 cases ONLY 8 OUNCES
Petit beurre Cookies 6 boxes BROKEN COOKIES ARE UNEXCEPTABLE
Johnny Walker Red and Black 2 cases of each
Absolute Vodka 2 cases
Benson and Hedges cigarettes 6 cartons ULTRA LIGHTS
Chocolate Pretzels 2 dozen NO BROKEN ONES
Ben & Jerry ice cream N.Y. Super Chunk 3 pints
I need a lot more things but these I need A.S.A.P.
        Michelle

There were some astronomical amounts of products on that list. That couldn't be right; who could require this much crap in one house at one time, with only two people living in it?

With this list I figured I needed to make more than just a few stops, including, but not limited to, the supermarket, the liquor store, and the pharmacy. The pharmacy was for the cigarettes. I was informed that they had a house account set up there and by the looks of things, they needed it.

It was my first shopping expedition and it took up most of the afternoon. I felt like such an idiot buying all that crap. I must have looked like a bomb shelter chef, walking around in my uniform and carrying those large quantities of toilet paper, smokes, and booze.

I finally got back to the house, and before I started to put away the groceries a few of my many questions were about to be answered. Francis had informed me that the Mr. and Mrs. were waiting to talk with me. This, I thought, should be interesting.

I was led through a labyrinth of rooms and halls. Walls were overlaid in wondrous silk tapestries or decorated with framed oil paintings and pastel drawings, all originals no doubt. Polished hardwood floors were partly covered with hand-woven oriental rugs, and I saw antique furniture adorned with all sorts of vases and gold-rimmed picture frames. Large chandeliers and recess lighting illuminated the rooms. One room we passed through was a tribute to modern technology. It had a 64-inch flat screen high-definition TV, with surround sound and DVD capabilities. There was a full bar in the corner of the room, about 20 feet from the pool table, and wraparound plush sofa, two recliners, and circular wooden coffee table completed the room's setting. Further down the hall I passed by an indoor greenhouse. It looked like a tropical garden. Green leaves, vines, and flowers of all colors were bursting through the tinted glass. Then I passed by an office, oops, make those two offices, and finally the tour stopped in a spacious room. It was decorated entirely in all sorts of reds with a large fountain in the middle of the room that cascaded red water from out its spouts. Blood-red silk lace flowed down the walls, and crimson carpets with intricate patterns were under my working-class feet.

I was told to sit down and wait for them. Of course, the antique couch my unworthy ass sat down on was clothed in a soft shade of cerise and the satin throw pillows were in scarlet red. I waited a few minutes in a room that was giving me flashbacks of a bad acid trip or seemed like a setting from "The Shining." As the minutes passed I was starting to get antsy, so I lifted the lid of an antique box on the cherry wood end table to see it was filled with cigarettes. A dull red disposable Bic lighter looked out of place next to the box, but hey, every room has its weakness. In the near distance I heard footsteps, and I figured this must be them.

Lo and behold entered the couple. Charm and grace exuded from the lady of the house. Wavy auburn brown hair hung midway down her back. She had a pretty face despite the excessive eye shadowing, which was an odd shade of blue. She had the figure of a model... or a famine victim, take your pick. It wouldn't be hard to examine her bone structure through the tight-fitting sequin garb that barley covered her breasts. Mrs. B was certainly a sexy broad, refined and smart looking; she looked about 45 years old and was coddling a rocks glass as she entered the room. She sat down first and smiled, half like Greta Garbo and half like the Grim Reaper, which had a chilling effect. Then it dawned on me… was she the Queen of Cups I was to beware of? She couldn't be; she didn't look at all like someone to beware of. In fact, she looked a lot better than bad. I never had a boss that looked even half that good. Hell, the only cups she seemed to be queen of was the A cups, which I could clearly see.

Mr. B stumbled in as cumbersome as she was graceful. Immediately, I took him for a reincarnation of W.C. Fields. His nose was the splitting image, Rudolph-red and bumpy. The rest of him also fit the bill: a round, slightly balding head that was also an uncomfortable shade of red. His body was rotund, not fat, but he could stand to lose a few pounds. He was dressed in a business suit and wore a gaudy amount of jewelry on his stubby fingers and wrists. One of the rings had a mothball-sized diamond protruding from the solid gold band; it had to be the biggest diamond I had ever seen. He sat down on the couch next to his wife; actually, he plopped into it as if he had bowling balls in his pockets. Some of his drink splashed out onto his suit. He did not seem too concerned about the stains on his suit. Instead he immediately called Francis for a refill. Mrs. B also called for a refill of her Absolute on the rocks. I was just hoping for a plastic cup of tap water, but nothing was offered.

"What is your name, boy?" Mr. asked, sharply.

"His name is Bob, you know that," his wife jumped in.

"Oh, Bob, that's right. So Bob, have you been cooking long?" he slurred.

"He's been cooking for years, dear, remember we talked about this." She was obviously losing patience with his questions.

"Actually, my name is Brian, and yes, I have been cooking for some time," I chimed in.

"I said Brian, didn't I dear," Mrs. B responded, obviously displeased with being corrected.

"Who cares, Bob, Brian, Brian, Bob. He's getting paid, and that's all that matters, right?" he said, answering his own question with a pompous look on his face. "More scotch, Francis!" he bellowed, not realizing Francis had already filled his glass. If they kept up this pace I'd need to go to the liquor store again, as soon as tomorrow.

"So, you understand, Bob, we want things done a certain way," he went on. "Mrs. B will discuss the menus with you, and we won't stand for any trouble. We prefer you to keep the business of the house to yourself. No guests are allowed on the premises. No long-distance calls, nothing leaves the property without our permission, you understand?" Mr. B. said, nodding yes to me as he polished off the rest of his scotch.

"So what do you think of the house? Impressed?" he asked to the air. "You bet your ass you are."

Mr. B seemed to have the annoying habit of answering his own questions.

He continued. "There are items in this house that are worth well over a million. Maybe if you're lucky, I'll take you for a spin in one the cars."

He was starting to slur his words a bit. Mrs. B took notice.

"You better stop your drinking," she said, appearing peeved. "You drink much too much, and I don't want him in my car. Nothing personal," she assured me.

"I understand," I said. *I understand you're nuts, lady*, I thought to myself.

"Francis, another one," Mr. B beckoned.

Mrs. B rose from her seat, apparently annoyed with her husband, and started to walk out of the room. She stopped at the doorway.

"Any questions, Bob?" she asked. "Good," she responded, before I had the chance to answer. "Oh, by the way, dinner will be at 8:00 p.m., tonight's my massage night." She said this like I knew all about massage night. "Mr. B is in the mood for lamb chops. Right, dear?" She looked in Mr.'s direction.

"Yes, certainly, that sounds fine," he answered as if she were his boss.

"We like them medium rare, not rare, not well, but medium-rare," she told me, as if the difference eluded me. "Oh, make a couple extra for the dogs, without the seasoning.

Ta ta," she concluded with a short wave, and left the room.

This left me alone with Mr. B. He leaned back a little deeper into the couch, appearing more comfortable with his wife's departure. He lifted his drink up to eye level, momentarily becoming fixated on its contents. He eyed the glass as if it contained a hidden message or possibly a stock tip. He gave the glass a slight twirl and then all in one shot, poured its contents down his throat. He abruptly placed the glass on the cocktail table and with every ounce of strength he possessed, pushed himself up from the couch. He lumbered over to the doorway, using both hands to hold him upright, then slyly peeked around the corner.

"She's gone, thank God," he mumbled to himself. "Come on, boy." He motioned for me to follow him.

He led me on a much different direction through the house from the way Francis showed me. I thought I was going to get a secondhand buzz from the alcohol fumes exuding from his body. Can a person get a contact high from the smell? I remember thinking that this guy must be pickling himself from the inside out. With all that booze, his liver must be enormous.

When we reached the front door, the Mr. opened a small drawer in an antique table in the hallway, extracted two small airplane-sized bottles of scotch, stuffed them in his pocket, and motioned for me to follow him outside.

"Which one of these beauties do you want to take out?" he asked me when we finally arrived at the garages. "Hop in and I'll take you for a ride." He slurred his words just enough to make me nervous about getting into any of the cars with him.

"I um, uh, don't really know," I stammered, shrugging my shoulders, because I didn't really want to go.

"The maz, one of the merc's? You name it, boy," he prompted.

"How about that big one?" I said, pointing to a large, shiny SUV that I'd never seen before. I thought it would be the safest in case he wrapped us around a tree.

"Whatever," he said as he fought to get his large body into the small red Maserati, showing absolutely no interest in the car I had suggested. If I hadn't been so afraid for my life I might have laughed at such a wild scene. I took a deep breath a climbed in.

He backed the car out and proceeded out of the driveway, with barely a thought to the manicured lawn he was turfing or flowerbeds he was plowing through. It was the first and last time I had ever used anything but the servant's entrance in or out of the property. He shot toward the heavy iron gates, hardly giving them time to open before he raced down the street.

"So, where to?" he said a few minutes and a couple of traffic violations later.

"Maybe the supermarket?" I answered, thinking it would be the easiest and fastest place to go. Plus, I did need to get the lamb chops for dinner. "I was at the store earlier today, but your wife just told me you wanted lamb a few minutes ago," I said carefully, testing my boundaries with the Mr.

"Can you believe this car?" he half-asked, half-yelled at me. He was looking at me like I had three heads or something because I wasn't slobbering all over his Euro-trash car. Or maybe he really was seeing three heads in his inebriated state, who knew?

He screeched into the supermarket's parking lot, nearly hitting another car before parking in a handicap spot, on a diagonal.

"Here, take this," he said, reaching into his wallet for some money.

I didn't know what to say after he handed me a crisp one hundred-dollar bill, so I just walked toward the store. Before I reached the entrance I glanced back at the car, still somewhat surprised that I was still in one piece. I watched him drain one of the liquor bottles.

I was lucky that the butcher still had some nice Colorado racks left for me, but I guessed that the $29.99 per pound cost might have had something to do with it. I grabbed a few, not forgetting to get extra for the dogs, and went back to my sloshed employer. He didn't say a word to me the entire ride home. Maybe he was infuriated at my lack of interest in his dumb car. I didn't care as long as he got us home safe, and sure enough, within minutes we were pulling up to his house with no problem. He parked right in front of the house, got out, and walked in without even a backwards glance in my direction. I was left standing there with the lamb chops in my hand, not really understanding what had happened, until I realized he wanted me to walk around back to the kitchen entrance. My God, was my opinion really all that important to him? Was he so impressed with himself that he needed everyone around him to be equally so? If that was the case, then I blew it big time, but I was never into cars and things like that and even less into pretending that I was. The Mr. must have realized that because he never again showed me any of his pretty things.

So… that was it. I finally met the B's.

Roast Rack of Lamb
Red Wine Mashed Potatoes
Baby Vegetables

I pour a few half-empty red wine bottles into a pot, along with a few sprigs of thyme and a pinch of sugar. I put this on the stove to reduce slowly. The end result is red wine syrup, intense with flavor.

The chops are big and meaty. The butcher cleaned them for me, taking off the silver skin, excess fat, and he **frenched** the bones for added appearances. The lamb meat has an excellent flavor, so I simply season liberally with kosher salt and fresh ground pepper. I **sear** the chops in a hot pan with olive oil. As they are becoming nice and brown, a sprig of rosemary is thrown in for good luck. The searing of the meat provides a tasty crust that helps the lamb retain its luscious juices. I allow the chops to cool on a rack while I work on the other items.

Large Idaho potatoes get set on a baking sheet. They are oiled and salted and placed into the oven for about an hour. After they are cooked all the way through, I cut them in half and remove the potato. I place the steaming hot starch into a **food mill** and turn the crank. Over a bowl the food mill drops the smoothed potato. I season the potato with salt and pepper and add some hot heavy cream and butter. I don't add too much because the red wine syrup is going to be added next, and too much liquid will make the potatoes too loose. The syrup turns the albino mashed potatoes to a deep burgundy. The red wine and thyme reduction adds great depth to the roasted potato flavor. I've found that roasting the potatoes and then mashing makes for a much better end product. I wrap the bowl in saran wrap and let it sit on a pot of simmering water to keep it from getting cold.

The lamb chops are ready for a hot 450-degree oven. Before they go in the oven, I wrap foil around the bones so they don't get black and brittle. I put them in for 15 to 18 minutes for a desirable medium-rare. The unseasoned racks for the dogs are also going in.

While the lamb is cooking, I prep up the veggies. Baby vegetables nowadays come in all sorts of cool varieties. I bought some yellow **pattypans**, green zucchinis, and baby carrots. I quickly peel the tender carrots and drop them into some boiling salted water. A minute or two later I drop the other vegetables. Spacing here is needed because not all of these guys cook at the same rate.

When they are done al dente (get used to that phrase), they are tossed into a butter sauce. To make this butter sauce, I combine a touch of white wine with water that has been seasoned and brought to a boil. Slowly, I add a few tablespoons of whole butter and whisk the mixture until it gets thick. Don't boil this mixture after this point. This **emulsion** will break, or separate, if boiled. The veggies are drained well so as not to dilute the butter sauce, and then they're tossed in a bowl with enough to coat each vegetable. The great thing about this butter sauce, besides the flavor, is that it will make the vegetables glisten because of its coating properties.

The lamb racks must cool for a good 5 minutes before being cut. This waiting period allows the juices to flow back into their veins and not flow all over the cutting board. The moment before cutting I brush a thin mixture of Dijon mustard, honey, and fresh lemon over the chops to pump up the already delicious flavor. With the first cut I can see the pink delectable flesh of the lamb. Each rack is cut into four two-bone chops.

I put a portion of potatoes on the middle of the plate. Two portions of meat are leaned up against the potatoes, so the bones are vertical. I drizzle some of lamb's pan dripping around the plate, and position the baby vegetables around the plate as well. A sprig of rosemary garnishes the plate, but I conveniently leave the garnish off the plate of chops meant for the dogs.

Little did I realize that my days would continue to be filled with a variety of peculiar situations, situations that I never could have imagined and would have an even a harder time explaining. Trying to get sympathy from my wife at first proved pointless—she was firmly optimistic and dismissive of my early concerns about my new job. She desperately wanted me to like this job. She loved my hours, and she loved the fact I wasn't coming home stinking of fried foods and beer. She especially loved the fact I did all my uniform laundry at the job (she hated the smell of my dirty chef clothes and said they stunk up the whole house). So it was only natural for my wife not to totally believe me when I told her about my joyride with Mr. B. I shouldn't have been so surprised. I mean, I barely believed it. Beth accused me of exaggerating and said that it was probably an innocent misunderstanding. Beth couldn't or wouldn't accept the fact that a rich and successful businessman would drive his expensive sports car around town shortly after polishing off almost a full bottle of scotch. Nor could she accept that I sat by myself in their kitchen for two hours with nothing to do, waiting for the Mrs. to finish her massage so I could cook their dinner.

More importantly, I could never get used to the lack of feedback on the meals I prepared. Francis would salivate, just hoping I would inquire on the B's contentment with the meals. He was quick at coming up with hurtful responses in an attempt to slowly chip away at my self-confidence. Not once can I recall him coming back from the dining room with two empty plates saying, "They loved everything" or "Complements to the chef." On the contrary, all my nights ended in just about the same way:

no recognition from the B's, no amicable conversation with Francis, and, ultimately, no hope for change.

CHAPTER EIGHT

"*THE GREATEST PLEASURE FOR A DOG IS that you may make a fool of yourself to him...*" wrote Samuel Butler, confirming what I now believe. How naive I must have been to buy into this whole "man's-best-friend" bullshit. Some dogs, particularly sheepdogs, have us humans pegged for complete suckers. As pet owners, we squander away our hard-earned money and precious time just to keep our canine companions healthy and happy. Sure, we get the odd tail wags and sloppy licks from our four-legged friends, but as I found out the hard way, some of these dogs take full pleasure in making us jump through hoops and play fetch. After working for these two dogs (and I do mean working for), I came to the conclusion that these sheepdogs of the rich and famous had me eating right out of their paws.

Anthony and Cleopatra are names usually suited for kings and queens, or Shakespearean characters, but not in this case. Their names fit right in with their temperaments. The only props lacking were a crown and a tiara to complete this utterly insane doggie utopia. They were simply not your average house pets. Not too many dogs I know had a chauffeur to escort their hairy bodies to a personal groomer every other week. In fact, not too many people I know period, hairy or not, got that amount of grooming maintenance. I'm not talking about your regular flea and tic dip: these dogs got the works. A thorough shampooing was followed by a cut, blow-dry, and full pedicure or manicure (I'm not exactly sure what term a paw falls under). They even got dental work, including brushing and flossing. I sure wish I could have been on their health plan. But this was just the tip of the pampering iceberg for these majestic mutts.

When I took this job, I assumed I was to be a personal chef for just the two residents of the house as well as the occasional guests and dinner party invitees. Little did I know the dogs' appetites would factor so highly in the course of my day. To say that these canines ate better than most of the general public would be a gross understatement. The meal specifications that the Mrs. mandated for their daily consumption were very specific.

Only bottled water was allowed to be poured into their drinking bowls, and on very hot days, a few ice cubes were to be added to sufficiently quench their thirst. The dog food was quite a gastronomic fanfare; the dry food was certainly no inferior kibbles and bits, god forbid. A comprehensive blending, done by the most prestigious veterinarians and dog dieticians of our time, had created the perfect mixture, one for premium health, fine coat, and superior energy. Personally, I thought it was a bunch of bullshit, just another way to spend a lot of money. At $3.75 an ounce, you bet your bottoms they were dropping some serious cash for these tender vittles.

The dry food made up half of the equation; the other half was where I came in. An alternating menu consisting of beef, chicken, lamb, or tuna got mixed with the dry food they ate twice a day. Beef is a broad term, so lets narrow it down a bit. Prime rib, roasted on the bone, cooked to medium rare. These were bite-sized chunks of tender beef, cleaned of any trace of fat or gristle. Perdue chicken was acceptable, but they preferred I cook them a free-range bird from Lancaster, Pennsylvania. The chickens were poached whole and then carefully picked from neck to wing of all edible meat. "No bones, no bones about it," the Mrs. liked to say, her weak attempt at seeming anecdotal, when what she really meant was no bones or no job. The one good thing about poaching the chicken was that it produced a tremendous amount of kick-ass chicken broth.

The lamb meat was from the sirloin and was ground fresh by the butcher. The butcher would joke, "Is this for mousaka or shepherd's pie?" knowing full well that it was meant for the dogs. He got a big laugh at my expense. The meat got sautéed, a la taco meat, and it seemed to be the dog's favorite. The tuna was grade A, the best available—not even the best sushi bar could claim a fresher product. No way in hell could I just open a can of Star-Kist. This beautiful fish got poached and flaked into medium-sized pieces. Their food had to be warmed and then served in his and her gold-plated dog dishes, which had their names hand-painted in silver along the outside. Like all spoiled rotten dogs, they got their fair share of treats. I had to make homemade dog bones, I'm certainly not proud to say, as well as bone-shaped cookies, and occasionally a couple scoops of vanilla ice cream. Francis served the ice cream to them in the dining room. I think he hated doing it almost as much as I loved watching him do it.

Besides the grooming and elaborate meal plan, they had a personal trainer that came twice a week to teach obedience and to basically play a glamorized game of fetch. Although she would never admit it, the personal dog trainer claimed it was to check their heart rate and flexibility or some crap like that. Maybe she just thought I was born yesterday, or that I dropped down to this planet from a place where people speak no bullshit, but no one can tell me that a ball being thrown down a hill and then retrieved by a dog isn't, in fact, FETCH.

So this concludes the dog's dossiers. It sure gave me a new meaning to the old phrase of "living the dog's life."

CHAPTER NINE

It had been two and a half months since I started the job and I thought I was finally starting to develop a consistent routine. My workweek consisted of six days on and one day off. My original deal with the old chef, who incidentally, I haven't heard from since he offered me the job, was that I would have two days off a week. Somewhere along the line I accrued an extra workday, but I let it slide because I didn't feel comfortable saying anything to the B's. I had an overriding tendency to let my bosses get the best of me and at the same time was doomed to keep my emotions and opinions all bottled up. I know this is probably not the healthiest way to live one's life. All I have to do is look back over my track record and this flaw in my character is proven to be true over and over again.

I believe people can be broken down into two animal-like categories: lions and camels. The lion is the king of his domain, with a sense of pride, projecting outwardly a confident demeanor. It's hard to train the lions; they are independent and forthright, and they make it known to others where they stand. If pushed past that point, lions have no problems growling and, if need be, attacking. These people don't let problems fester to the point of ulcers and high-blood pressure. In high-stress occupations like the restaurant business, being a lion is not a bad thing. The camel, on the other hand, is a much more docile creature. It is bred for hard traveling and burden. It holds everything in, like the essential water supply it carries in its hump, hoping it will last until its master allows him to refill. Here, the old adage rings true; just one more straw will ultimately be the insignificant weight that breaks his back. I was like the camel, there's no doubt about it.

Maybe that was why I was hired? The chef must have had the foresight to see me as the ideal applicant for the job. He must have felt that I could be properly assimilated into this bizarre world without much resistance. I'm really not a complete pushover, but I would sooner be reincarnated as a rug than a bridge. I just seem to take it and take it, until finally I explode. This anger usually marks the end of the professional relationship with my current employer, and there you have my untenured resume. So, I let the extra day off slide, not because I didn't want or need it—on the contrary, that extra day off would have meant the world to me. It would have at the very least given me added home time with my kids, and it would have also shut Beth up. Having a set schedule and two days off was one of the reasons she wanted me to take this job. She hated the fact that I didn't say anything to the B's. She thought it was unfair, and let's face it, it *was* unfair. The reality was that if the B's had their way, I would have worked every day of the week. Family time? They could care less about my family time; the only family time that mattered was theirs. I once asked off for a Jewish holiday and they scoffed at my request. (Of course, it was denied in the form of a letter. Yes, a letter.) They needed me more than my God did, was basically their message.

But I was a camel, and for the time being my back was still holding the straws… but the straws were slowly starting to pile up. The one good thing the B's at least let me have was my one day off, which always fell on a Saturday, a day when my whole family was home.

Now back to the six days I was the B's property. I had broken each day down into three parts. The first was lunch. Most lunches I only had to cook for Mrs. B, except on Sundays and Mondays. Sunday was their family day; Mr. and Mrs. were both home, and lunches usually consisted of meals like:

Jumbo Lump Crab with asparagus, mango, and lemon vinaigrette
Or
Homemade thin crust pizzas topped with fresh mozzarella and basil
Or
Balsamic and Rosemary Chicken Paillard with Tucson White Bean Salad
Or
Poached Salmon with Potato Croquette and Remoulade Sauce

Their favorite meal was my quiche. It was the only dish they ever commented on. Except for the fact that I was still employed at the time, there was no discernable proof that they liked my cooking at all. I continued to ask Francis almost daily whether they liked everything after he cleared their plates, but as much as I continued to ask, he continued to be a dick about it. He would just remark, "Who cares?" or "Ask them yourself!" as he lit up a cigarette and blew the smoke out the side door. The Mrs. probably never realized it, but her nicotine addiction was a catalyst for Francis's. He smoked just as many (if not more) of the Mrs.'s cigarettes as she did, and that in itself was quite the feat. I could count on one hand how many times I saw her without a cigarette in her mouth.

It amazes me that the B's loved Francis so much, this guy who stole cigarettes from them. He was a lazy kiss-ass and quite frankly an insincere son of a bitch. He made comments to the B's that I never could have gotten away with, like complaining about his workload. I did think that he felt an extended privilege to treat me the way he did because he saw first-hand how the B's would do everything in their power to ignore me. So I guess he figured he didn't have to treat me any different than the B's did, especially since he was already so endeared to them. For whatever reason, it grew abundantly clear that Francis hated my guts, and it irked the hell out of me when he continually reminded me to buy more cigarettes for the Mrs. when I knew that I was really buying them for him. Let's just call it another straw on my back. I wouldn't mind exploding on him; that jerk deserved it.

So, as I was saying, the B's weren't ones for positive reinforcement. It would have been nice to know if they liked or disliked something so I could or could not repeat it. But the quiche must have certainly tickled their fancies because they asked for it many times.

Spinach, Tomato, and Comte Cheese Quiche
With Turkey Canadian Bacon

A homemade pie dough isn't essential but with one, your options for the quiche are greatly increased. The pre-made supermarket ones are usually cracked and have a couple broken pieces in the crust. With a homemade dough the ability to line a bigger mold and produce a fancier crust is just part of the advantage. The homemade variety will undoubtedly taste better, because you use whole butter instead of the shortening in the store bought and add spices and herbs for better flavor. I like to put fresh chervil and dill in mine for this recipe. My pie dough procedure is simple, one that also can be used for many other menu ideas, such as pot pies, fruit-filled pies, and tarts.

Pâte brisée is a buttery and flaky dough that will brown evenly and melt right in your mouth. Basically it's just a fancy French phrase for pie dough and the best thing about it is that the dough freezes excellently. It is mandatory for me to have pie dough ready to go in the freezer; you might think about doing the same. It will thaw quickly on the counter top, usually just in time to get the other ingredients ready. Plus a cold pie dough is the ideal temperature to work with and bake with. The butter in the dough when colder will make a better-textured piecrust because it will take longer to melt in the oven. When the butter gets hot, the water properties in the butter produce steam. The steam helps separate the individual layers in the pastry, which will create a flaky texture. If the dough is warm to start, the butter will steam to rapidly causing the pastry to overexpand, then shrink and become misshapen, plus the texture will suffer. I like to line the expensive Williams and Sonoma oversized, fluted, and ceramic baking dish with the dough, which has been rolled out to about 1/8-inch thick. Then I brush Dijon mustard on the dough with a pastry brush and put the dish in the freezer to chill for a few minutes. When properly chilled, the dough goes into a 350-degree oven for about 5 to 7 minutes. This will help brown the crust a bit but more importantly prevent the quiche from being soggy on the bottom; no one likes a soggy bottom. The mustard adds flavor and helps weigh the crust down so it won't rise when pre-baking. Some chefs use a term called blind baking, which is foil and beans in the crust to keep it from rising, but I prefer the mustard, and a very cold pie-shell.

Next is the batter, which I keep the same no matter what ingredients I use to flavor the quiche. I whip 3 eggs and a 1/2-pint of light cream. For this quiche pan I need to times the recipe by two because of its larger size. This recipe works perfect for a 9-inch pan. Reserve the egg-cream mixture off to the side while preparing the other ingredients.

Comte cheese is a hard Gruyere-style cheese made in France using cow's milk. It has an ivory to yellow interior and a golden brown rind with a slightly fruity and earthy flavor that provides an exquisite flavor to this dish. Just grate a chunk or two of the cheese with a box-grater. I prefer to use a lot of hearty ingredients in my quiche and rely less on the egg-cream mixture to fill the shell.

Spinach is a wonderful addition to many recipes. I prefer the larger, grown-up variety than the baby spinach because it will hold up better during the cooking process. Also because when I sauté the spinach after it is rinsed and stemmed it has the misfortune of shrinking down to scarce quantities, the baby more so than the mature variety. A little shallot is diced and added to a sauté pan and cooked with some olive oil until tender. Add the spinach and some salt and pepper, a touch of white wine to produce some steam, and the spinach should cook down in literally seconds. Let cool and reserve on the side, if possible (I like to put it in a sieve to let the excess liquid drain off). Too much extra liquid in the quiche could upset its consistency.

The tomatoes I use need to be prepared ahead. This element is probably the most time-consuming after the actual cooking time in the oven. I **monder** a few ripe plum tomatoes by simply taking out the core and marking the bottom of each tomato with a small X. The tomatoes are dropped into boiling water for 10 to 15 seconds, then immediately taken out and put on a plate and then into the refrigerator or let rest until cooled before the skin is to be peeled. I suggest this way opposed to shocking in cold ice water because it's my contention that the water will rob the tomatoes of some of their inherent flavor. After they are skinned, I cut the tomatoes in half lengthwise and gently squeeze some of the seeds out. I brush the tomatoes with olive oil and season lightly with salt and pepper and fresh thyme. The idea is to slowly roast the tomatoes in a 300-degree oven to let the flavors enhance and grow more intense, which usually takes about a half hour until the metamorphosis takes place. Let the roasted plum tomatoes cool and then cut into medium pieces.

The assembly of the quiche once all ingredients are ready is as follows.

Place some spinach, chopped tomato, and cheese in layers while adding the egg-cream mixture after each stage. Continue until the pan is just about full. Put the unbaked quiche in the oven for about 30 to 35 minutes. The ideal is a golden brown crust with the egg mixture just setting. Take the quiche from the oven and let set a good 5 minutes to allow the pie time to firm up.

The turkey Canadian bacon, an excellent product sold at one of the nearby farmer's markets on my route, is quickly browned on both sides in a cast-iron grill pan. A luscious wedge of quiche alongside of two grilled pieces of the bacon makes for an excellent Sunday lunch.

This recipe was a favorite of Mr. B on Sundays and the Mrs.'s secretary on Mondays. The secretary, Nancy, was a pleasant lady, and I didn't mind cooking for her at all. She was appreciative and sometimes even asked me for a recipe from the meal she ate. Now you might ask, what the hell does a secretary do for a woman who doesn't own a business or work at all for that matter? Believe me, I asked myself the same question plenty of times. I soon found out that Nancy basically just cleaned up the pile of crap on the Mrs.'s desk.

Nancy was great for a laugh though. She often admitted that it was such a joke, being paid to open mail and give opinions on shoe colors. Of course, she had much more important aspects to her job that shouldn't go unmentioned. She assisted in party preparations, such as checking off names on invitee lists, addressing invitations, and licking stamps. She also had the honor of making dinner reservations, booking vacations, sorting through receipts and junk mail, and folding down the corners of the more vital magazine pages so that the Mrs. had more time to do the important things in life, like shop.

Mondays usually meant a later lunch so I could put a little more time into the meal. The rest of the week it was mainly just the Mrs., lunch for one. She requested a steady diet of low-calorie meals to maintain her Olive Oyl-like physique. The Mrs. was a strong-minded individual; she was no dummy, so when she acted coy toward me, I knew she was pulling my chain. She loved playing games with me, and her favorite was the dinnertime guessing game. This was where I would ask what she wanted for dinner and she said, "I'll get back to you." Of course, I would have to ask again and again before I got an answer. It was embarrassing and demeaning to have to ask the same question over and over. She knew full well that I could easily choose an appropriate, tasty meal, but god forbid she didn't have full power over every household decision. She also loved to say, "Oh, Bobby dear, we might be going out to dinner tonight. I'll let you know." This totally put me in a holding pattern. Do I make dinner or not? If not, that meant I had to attempt to keep busy for hours, because if a private chef has no one to cook for then he really doesn't have anything to do. I often waited in the kitchen, sitting on the stool, watching the clock, praying for 5:00 p.m. so I could run out to my car and drive right into traffic. It seemed a lot better than sitting around being bored to death with nothing to do, letting my anger slowly build inside. It made me feel like such a loser to sit there, not knowing what was going on.

Francis and Michelle both reveled in my misfortune. They loved asking me what was for dinner, knowing as well as I that I had no idea. I couldn't even call Beth to tell her I was coming home early, not even at 4:59 p.m., because that was usually the magical time the epiphany of information happened to pop into the Mrs.'s head.

"Oh Billy darling," she would say over the intercom as I was preparing for a mad dash to my car. "We've decided to eat here, what did you have in mind for dinner?"

First of all, what I had in mind was that my fucking name is BRIAN, not Bobby or Billy. Second of all, did she really think that sitting on my ass for the last 3 hours in her kitchen contemplating suicide put me in any frame of mind to talk food, let alone start to create an elaborate three-course meal? Sadly, I played the role of sucker. I stuttered a bit before naming some choices, and not once did she bite on one of my recommendations anyway. She always would say, "Well, let me talk to Mr. B and see what he wants."

The aggravating thing was that she would make the decision anyway and I was just stuck in a purgatory of waiting until she felt merciful enough to clue me in. Sometimes she even waited an hour until she called down again.

"Bob dear, Mr. wants to go out to eat so we won't need you tonight after all." She'd say it as if she felt bad for making me wait around but it was the Mr.'s fault, that he was the one so undecided about dinner. I always found it funny how she would relay this newfound information to me when the house phone hadn't rang (she never used a cell phone). It was just her way of passing the time, a pleasant mode of torture to get her through her hard, grueling days. It must have been so difficult to get everything she wanted, to be waited on hand and foot and have her ass kissed so many times that it actually started to chap. Oh, the horrors of it all. Thank God I didn't have those problems; my ass just got chapped sitting like a damn fool in her damn kitchen.

CHAPTER TEN

My routine, beside the essential parts of cooking lunch and dinner for the Mr., Mrs., and the dogs, was filled with all sorts of mundane tasks. I did my own laundry, which included my uniforms and kitchen towels. Beth found it hilarious that I did the wash… she doesn't even allow me to come within three steps of the washer and dryer at home. But at the mansion… well, it was my responsibility to wash, dry, and fold everything I used in the kitchen. Other additional jobs included taking out the kitchen trash, maintaining both of the kitchen's dishwashers, and, my pet peeve, refilling the beverages in the refrigerator. There must have been full rows of every assortment of sodas and waters in the refrigerator at all times, yet it seemed like I was constantly restocking the refrigerator, even though I didn't drink anything from it. Francis drank about eight Cokes a day, and Michelle and Josie sucked down the diet beverages. You would have thought just once they would have refilled the refrigerator, seeing as though they were the ones drinking them. It was just another straw; I told myself it didn't bother me, but really it did.

If cooking wasn't my most important function, shopping would certainly have been. Sometimes I thought shopping was my most important duty, but I tried not to dwell on it because if I did then I'd really be depressed. Being a personal chef I could live with, but being a personal shopper… now that was another story. I had found that shopping for the B's was not an easy task. It was easier—wait, make that *much* easier—to shop (or really order) for restaurants than it was to keep up stock for these people.

Here's a little note I received one day. I found it lying on top of my cutting board first thing in the morning.

Dear Bob,

Michelle has informed me that YOU have refused her request to acquire more toilet paper. This isn't the first time. She has asked YOU to purchase supplies for the house before, and YOU have not complied. I told her to give YOU a chance because YOU were new, but now it's becoming a problem. I was hoping the two of you could work out the differences amongst yourselves. However, the house MUST be maintained and it's YOUR job to do the shopping. Michelle is only doing HER job. She is trying to keep a certain quantity of supplies in the house so we don't run short. In the future, I EXPECT YOU to buy everything she requests to satisfy the needs of the house.
Mrs. B

Each line of the note shoved my integrity down a notch, and I knew that the others read the letter, which really pissed me off. How about an envelope, or a freaking manila folder? Did every pathetic iota of this humiliating job have to be public knowledge amongst the other commoners? I was a loser. I had to be to work there. I knew this, but as the immortal Bob Dylan sang, "You have to serve somebody," so these are the somebodies I had to serve. Let's face facts, money doesn't grow on trees, at least not in my backyard, so I had to be a responsible adult and work for a living. But back to my real duress, why did my misfortunes have to be public knowledge? Mrs. B was a conniving, plotting, diabolical witch! That had to be the answer. Why else would she embarrass me over toilet paper? We are talking toilet paper, for Christ's sake! How much toilet paper does one skinny women need, anyway? Did I miss something? Was there a toilet paper shortage? Was the U.S.

under attack? Come on! Give me a fucking break. It's not like I covertly took the job, put up with sycophant employees, cooked for dogs, and succumbed to the whims of two eccentric billionaires all to unleash my diabolic plot to have Mrs. B wipe her pristine ass with torn newspapers and rocks. She found me out! That's right, I went to college for 4 years and suffered through this business for another 10 years all to give this woman a proper ass chaffing. I've been exposed! I guess the three 9-pack Charmins I bought the day before that were probably still in the upstairs closet weren't enough to get her through the night. Not to mention the seven other bathrooms throughout the house that had an average of 3 to 4 rolls in each one. Let's see, I'm no math major but 3 x 9 plus 4 x 7 equals 55. A grand total of 55 rolls of toilet paper were in this house at that exact moment, give or take some squares. What was this, a subway station? Did we have a sign outside posted on the front grounds saying, "Come wipe your dirty ass here!"

I later found out that Mrs. B supposedly used an entire roll of toilet paper *per session*, all while wearing latex gloves to keep her germophobic mind at ease. God forbid any fecal matter fell on her milky white hands. Come on, lady! Ease up on the t.p. and maybe the plumber wouldn't have to come and unclog the pipes every other day. How many times in a day did can the woman shit? I guess with the laxatives she took after each meal six trips to the bathroom a day was a fair number. This lady was a pooping machine. Christ, on a good coffee-and-doughnut day I might go three, four times. But with all this said, wouldn't 55 rolls of toilet paper per day set even the most manic mind at ease? Oh well, life's a crapshoot. I guess I would be shopping for toilet paper that day, along with the rest of my ever-growing list.

My shopping excursions had become legendary. I had discreetly deemed that portion of my job "my route." The route consisted of the pursuit of various goods from numerous outlets in a 30-mile radius around the B's. I had developed relationships with fellow shoppers and was on a first-name basis with a myriad of retailers in the area. From grocery store clerk to stock boy to the local pharmacist, from specialty shop managers to liquor store supervisor, even the girl at the pet store knew my name. There was a higher status given to me, as the term regular was something of an understatement. For example, at the supermarket, it wasn't unusual for a checkout line to be surreptitiously opened as I completed my shopping. Nor was it an accident that the private bathroom key in one supermarket was conveniently in my possession. It was a form of respect I guess... maybe not the stuff dreams are made of, but at least it was something. For me, going to the same store twice, even three times a day wasn't unheard of. The Mrs. could and did change her mind quite often throughout a day on what she wanted for dinner. So basically I bought and brought every commodity that was to come into the house. I was, in essence, the house errand boy.

On one occasion, I was asked to pick up some rare art supplies that only a particular shop carried. I think they were imported pastels from France that contained just the right hues. Anyway, the shop was located on a busy road that was loaded with tiny shops and stores. Between the heavy traffic and the tiny, hard-to-read signs, I was experiencing difficulty in locating the store. The whole time I was nervous because back at the house I had a pot of Irish Stew on the stove for dinner. I only had so much time to be out on my route to begin with before dinner was ruined. I was picturing the cast-iron pot, the stew delicately bubbling, distinct aromas perfuming the empty kitchen with scents of rosemary, thyme, and juniper berry. This was one dinner that needed to be started before my daily shopping trip began. If not, the meal would never be ready for dinnertime.

As each moment passed and as each store and street sign receded, I was starting to get an uncomfortable feeling that I had passed the art store. In the back of my mind I could see the stew that I worked so hard on just burning away because of a few fucking French pastels. Like

American pastels couldn't do the trick? Or how about Mrs. B getting her thonged ass out in this traffic to hunt down these elusive implements! Somewhere between looking to the right and squinting my eyes toward the left, I failed to notice the traffic light turning from yellow to red. In my defense, I was trailing a truck with an oversized cargo-haul that obstructed my vision, so I never stood a chance. As I proceeded through the intersection, a light-blue Chevy plowed right into the side of my vehicle. My head was already pressed up against the windshield giving me optimum viewing for this damn store so it had little space to travel to impact against the hard glass. My body then flung back into the driver's seat with whip-lash movement. The SUV I was driving was pushed up onto two tires and continued "James Bond Style" through the intersection for about 20 feet. Not until I slammed on the breaks did it stop and fall back on its four tires.

I was seeing stars, and then I was seeing an older gentleman screaming at me outside my car door. My fuddled brain surmised that this must be the driver of the blue Chevy that hit me. The man obviously wasn't injured in the accident, but he was sure pissed off. Between the barrage of expletives and his broken car horn blaring non-stop, there was quite a racket. I was developing quite a stress headache on top of my slight concussion. I got out of the car and grimaced at the site of the crumpled-in driver's side door, two flat tires, and bent rims. This was not a good thing.

And the stew! What was to become of the stew? I guess with the current situation being as it was, a potentially burning stew would be the last thing on someone's mind, but not me. The stew was my main concern, for cooking was the only reason I stayed at this crazy position. It was my main responsibility, not the procuring of pastels, for Christ's sake. The only problem with my pretzel logic is that I didn't realize the B's wouldn't see it quite the same way.

The police came and did the usual accident scene formalities. They listened to my version, then they listened to the other guy's version, and then they handed me my own copy of the police report. It was more than a little embarrassing having to call Francis, but I had to do it. I could hear the amusement in his voice as I heard him loudly broadcasting my story back at the house.

"You got in an accident!" he was screaming on the other end. "It was your fault? What, the car is not drivable?"

What could I do? I was at his mercy, but I sure didn't receive any. He did pick me up on the side of the road an hour later, where I sat on the curb with a few grocery bags, my skull violently throbbing. I waived goodbye to the mangled cars as they were towed away and watched the traffic get back to normal. Francis had a lit cigarette in his hand and a smug expression on his face.

"You're fucked," he smiled, and then he offered me one of the Mrs.'s cigarettes. What a sport. I lit up the cigarette and leaned back, exhaling a deep breath. "Don't worry about it, it's only a car, they can afford it, believe me." He said, sounding almost like a human being.

He told me that Josie turned the stew off and not to worry about anything. I frowned to myself. Was I dreaming? Was I delirious from the crash? Was he actually cutting me some *slack* or something? As I sat in the passenger seat I realized that what was occurring was actually a minor bonding experience. Maybe, just maybe, deep down, he hated the B's as much as I did, but he kissed so much ass that his lips were permanently stuck in a puckered hell.

We pulled into the driveway, and as I got out of the car a pain shot through my back to match the pain in my head. I carried the groceries into the house and dropped them on top of the kitchen island. The Mrs. was there in the kitchen waiting for me, and before I could say a word she spoke.

"I hope you at least picked up the pastels," she said matter-of-factly as she puffed on a cigarette. I sadly shook my head no. From her pinched expression I knew I was in for a real treat now. She crushed out her cigarette, lit another, and stared at me for what seemed like an eternity. She finally sighed and said, "So what happened?"

Three renditions and four cigarettes later she still hadn't asked me if I was hurt or if I wanted to go to the hospital or, gasp, go *home* for the rest of the day. Instead, she was more interested in knowing whether I gave my insurance card to the officer or the one in the SUV's glove box. I pretended not to hear her for a while, trying to stop myself from flipping out on her. I still can't believe I didn't snap. The car was technically a company car used only for work, and I wasn't out on a freaking joy ride! Of course I didn't use my personal car insurance information! She had a lot of nerve, even more nerve than I had thought.

She got up from her chair to leave the room and simply said, "Dinner will be at 7:00 p.m., and don't forget to keep the Mr.'s pearl onions on the side."

So there I was, left standing alone in the kitchen, in quite a bit of pain. With my whole body shaking and shivering, the dogs started stalking me for their dinner, and I basically felt like a poster child for abused servants. I was left with only one thing to do, one chance to salvage what was left of my diminishing dignity. The Irish stew. This was going to be the best damn stew I ever made.

Irish Lamb Stew

Tender morsels of lamb enriched by a hearty broth laden with vegetables, herbs, and wine. "Comfort food" is a term given to dishes that can warm both the heart and belly, and this meal certainly falls under that category.

Stews have always been a favorite of mine. They evoke in me an unbridled passion towards perfecting them. Making a lamb stew is, in the simplest of terms, a labor of love. Even though I started this dish earlier in the day, I will describe the dish as if I am starting at the present moment.

The meat is from Jamison Farms, an excellent purveyor of high-quality lamb products. For this dish I recommend leg meat because the leg meat provides some of the finest and richest flavors lamb has to offer. Like most animal meat, you will discover better tasting meat from areas of the body that get more exercise and daily use. The added movement in these muscles creates more connective tissue development, which gives the meat added flavor, but also causes the meat to have added toughness. A slow-cooking process or a stewing method must be used to break down the meat, but the results certainly make it worthwhile. The leg meat, cut into chunks, is tossed in flour that has been seasoned with salt, black pepper, thyme, ground juniper berries, and chopped rosemary. I sear each piece of meat on all sides in a large cast iron pot using olive oil and a medium-high flame. The searing will keep in all the juices while creating a flavorful crust. The meat is transferred out of the pot and set on the side. In the meantime, to the pot with the essence of lamb clenched firmly to its bottom, I add chopped garlic, tomato **concassee,** fresh rosemary, and thyme. Ever so briefly I swirl the ingredients around the heated pot, stopping only slightly to take in the delightful fragrances. Next comes a proper deglazing of Beaujolais Village, a blend of wines from 39 communes in Beaujolais that has more body and flavor than the normal Beaujolais. And when I say proper, I mean a plentiful pour, about a whole bottle. I let the wine reduce and mingle with its new friends for a while, and after the new relationships are forged I add lamb **demi-glaze** to the pot. Back to the pot goes the lamb meat, ready to be tenderized by both the wine and ample cooking time. For about an hour the stew simmers; the flavors and texture become richer and richer. At this point I add lightly poached, whole Yukon gold potatoes, sweet medium-sized carrots cut oblique, and two to three 1-inch-sized ribs of celery. This all simmers for another 30 minutes. My desire is to have all the vegetables become tender simultaneously. I check for seasoning, add a dash of salt and pepper, and end with some fresh peas, a **chiffonade** of Italian parsley, and one nice shot of grated lemon rind.

In the B's case, a minor modification was required. Mrs. B would just die if any onion, shallot, or in this case, golden pearl onion passed through her system. I couldn't imagine the amount of toilet paper she would need if one were to find its way into her intestines. She's convinced they cause gas and she's not a big fan of the gas. So any delicate members of the onion family must be sautéed on the side for Francis to spoon into the Mr.'s bowl.

What a day! Its times like those when a paranoid euphoria took over my power of logical thinking. How could anyone this side of Murphy's Law be thrust into such a bizarre and embarrassing predicament? I've had my fair share of crappy days like anybody else, from brain surgeon to grease monkey, whale hunter to shoe salesman. I know that no matter the field, we all have our share of ups and downs. But the only caveat on my career stairway was the sense that the only possible direction I could have gone was straight up. This job couldn't have got any worse, it just couldn't. The job had already surpassed even my most heart-wrenching times of employment. I have never been treated as impolitely and insensitively as I had been at that house. The B's torturing techniques were unsurpassed. They took pleasure in both the turning of the screw approach to wearing down the self respect of their employees and simply treating us like second-class citizens right to our faces. They shared characteristics with such characters as Dr. Evil, Saroman, and the red-horned devil himself. I thought maybe there was some alien culture monitoring my ability to withstand pain and humiliation. I have swallowed my pride to legendary depths, fought down my urges to verbally explode and instead sat by, watching with my mouth wide open as I accepted all of their bullshit as I was slowly being turned into a mute, self-loathing loser. So, as I said, I felt that I had survived the worst and it definitely was the worst, and now I was hoping that the job could only get better.

CHAPTER ELEVEN

As I pulled up to my house after the car accident/lamb stew incident, I realized that I had forgotten to call my wife and inform her about my unfortunate circumstances that day. I guess it was entirely possible that she would have been slightly intrigued by my near-fatal car accident. Okay, so it wasn't near fatal, but the large bump on my head and my sore neck and back were no mirages. She was going to be pissed off that I didn't tell her about it sooner.

It only took her a second to tell something was wrong. "Brian, what the hell happened to you?" she said when she saw me, biting her lip, a pained expression on her face. "You are as pale as a ghost. And what's up with the bump on your forehead?"

Beth could always sense if I was hiding something and she certainly sensed something the moment I came through the door. Maybe my body language gave it away... the way I slumped through the doorway with an aching back and stiffened neck. I guess the audibly discernable groaning was also a dead giveaway, but what the hell, I needed the sympathy.

"Seriously, what's goin on?" she asked, her voice getting louder with each word. "You're starting to scare me."

I stumbled over to the sofa and awkwardly fell into the soft cushions, leaving my clogs where I stood. Nervously, Beth scooped them up, set them near the radiator by the front door, and came back over to me. Kneeling by my side, she positioned her body between my legs and held my one hand with two of hers.

"Are you going to tell me what happened?" she said very softly, looking solemnly into my sad, brown eyes.

"Well, you see, I kinda of, well..." I hung my head in shame, more embarrassed now, given the reality of having to tell my tale. Maybe embarrassed wasn't the right word. Maybe enraged would be more appropriate. Not at the B's, although no one could blame me if I were. I was basically mad at myself for not being able to put myself first. Hell, my *family* first. What would happen to them if I got seriously injured? How could I justify the fact that I let Mrs. B play the victim? I should have ripped her a new asshole, and if anyone could use an extra one, it would be her. I had blown my chance. I could have told Mrs. B that I was the one who was injured, not her, and if Irish stew was so important to her she could go buy two first-class tickets to Ireland and get a couple of hearty crocks there. But I didn't have the guts or the balls, so now... I had the guilt.

"Are you going to tell me what happened... or not?" Beth asked. "You are pale, you're not talking... Did you do something wrong?"

In a manner of speaking, yes, I did do something wrong. But I couldn't find the words. It seemed I was capable only of inner monologue, not conversation.

By this time the boys had scrambled down the stairs to greet their daddy. They ran past Mommy and fell into my arms. Mommy let go of my hand and began pacing the room.

"Daddy, guess what I did today?" Brooks exclaimed.

"What?" I responded with as much interest as I could muster.

Before he could answer, Beth asked them to go upstairs.

"Mommy and Daddy have something very important to talk about," she said, looking at me intently.

"You guys are going to kiss," the youngest boy stated. Daniel had such a very direct way of putting things.

Both boys were hysterically giggling and making pretend kissing noises as they ran up the stairs.

"We are *not* going to kiss!" Beth barked quite seriously after them.

"Never?" I uttered meekly.

"Goddamn it, it *will* be never if you don't tell me what happened!" she snapped. Her patience was gone.

I was in a pickle ... it just occurred to me, that makes no sense, shouldn't I have been in a pickle jar? No matter, Beth had smoke coming out of her cute little ears, which I may have never been able to nibble on again if I didn't tell her what happened. So I told her.

I told her about the art supplies, I told her about the accident, I told her about the kitchen scene with Mrs. B, and I told her about the stew. Well ... I tried to tell her about the stew.

"You know what, Brian?" she interrupted. "I am just a wife and mother. I try to do the best I can, and if that's not good enough... well then it's not good enough. You care way too much about what these people think when all they do is take you for granted. I was hoping this job would be different and maybe you could separate yourself from the job and spend more time with the family. But I can tell things aren't all that much better. I still have to be practically a single parent to two small boys, but also take care of the wounds you get everyday. I don't know what these rich assholes are doing to you, but it has to stop. Either quit or put your foot down about what you want."

I was beginning to wonder when she was going to take a break because my head was spinning even before she got started. Her rant continued. "Do you want to end up like all those couples we worked with? Divorced, bitter, and going to AA? You better start sticking up for yourself. You don't get paid nearly enough for either one of us to put up with this shit."

She finally finished and marched upstairs, leaving me alone with my throbbing head and dirty uniform. I slept on the couch that night, not moving until morning.

CHAPTER TWELVE

A WEEK OR SO AFTER MY CAR ACCIDENT I was standing in the kitchen at the mansion and in came two little Asian ladies. I didn't know where they came from… for all I knew they could have walked out of one of the B's exotic Oriental tapestries like a couple of Geisha beauties.

"Stop staring, it's rude!" Michelle exclaimed in my direction. "I'll have you know they come here every year for almost one whole day to show Mrs. B all the new styles from over in that Chinese place."

"Oh, I see. That clears it up," I replied sarcastically.

"You know that place called Tokie something, well I'm not sure exactly where, but they like tea and those message cookies, I do know that," Michelle said presumptuously.

Obviously Michelle had no problem wearing her lack of intelligence on her sleeve. Attempting to look like I wanted to give her my full attention, I leaned forward, resting my elbows on the kitchen island while resting my chin in my hands.

"Oh please, do go on," I urged. "I am just so impressed with your wealth of knowledge on this subject."

"You're impossible," she exclaimed, pushing her chair quite forcefully back under the island.

"What's wrong?" I asked. "I was just wondering if you could enlighten me further, or was that the extent of your expertise on Far Eastern culture?"

"Fuck you!" she snapped. "I'm sick of your Cheffy attitude." Her verbal assault was accompanied by her menacing buckteeth edging out past her bottom lip.

"Don't you mean Fook Yu," I said, trying to hold back my laughter. She continued to glare at me. "Oh come on Michelle, I'm just kidding," I said. "How about instead you can just fill me in on the origin of the chop-stick or at least analyze some Confucian principles for me," I called out after her as she started to leave the kitchen. "Wait, Michelle, where are you going? I'm trying to be serious ... don't leave."

By this point Michelle was halfway up the back steps, obviously angered by my obnoxious tone.

"How about soy sauce, any theories on that!" I yelled up the steps. "Chow!" I yelled even louder.

"Chow," said the two Asian ladies as they continued through the house carrying dresses, shoes, lacy undergarments, satin robes, and all sorts of cosmetics. Like a procession, they passed through the kitchen, through the breakfast room, through dining room, up the main staircase, and into the Mrs.'s private dressing room.

Josie ran after them to grab two boxes of rubber gloves from the supply closet in the mudroom. Mrs. B always made her clothing fitters wear protective gloves when they touched her or anything that was to touch her. And it wasn't just a one-day bigotry. Everybody from the Neiman Marcus employees to the metrosexuals from Sacks 5th Ave. needed to be armed with latex gloves before any fitting was to be done. She was prejudiced against all people equally.

The fact that I was seeing a couple of Asian ladies who flew a few thousand miles with their wares just to please this spoiled-rotten matron didn't surprise me in the least. With the large amount of cash she shelled out for clothing and accessories, I'm more surprised that a representative or two from every country didn't fly, sail, or swim over here to muscle in on some of this lucrative action. The fact that this lady upstairs saw nothing unusual about her private fittings killed me. In the real world, most women would never even dream of having even a K-Mart sales lady drive a few blocks with a bag full of the latest Jaclyn Smith line for someone to try on.

Michelle and Josie were busy with the Ladies for the rest of the day and I was informed that the Mr. and Mrs. would be eating out that evening… Chinese food no doubt.

Every day in that place I was faced with Mrs. B.'s realities and they would completely mess with my mind. What I used to think were universal truths about humanity were totally mixed up. I could feel myself slipping into some crazy place between both worlds. I knew I didn't belong in theirs but didn't feel good in my old place either. I was a hard worker, I came from a good family, I had advantages others never did, and yet I could never come close to what these people had. Nor could I grasp any sort of perspective that would satisfy my confusion of the fact that I was really playing a role in this mad play.

There simply was no line of inconvenience that Mrs. B wouldn't cross or, better yet, have someone else cross for her. Like the time she was late for Sunday morning mass and she wanted me to call the church to ask the Priest to delay Mass.

"Brian," she said in her unique way. "I am running a little late, so will you please phone the priest and ask him to wait for me." She said this as if it were no small request. I guess she figured that since she hadn't asked me to phone the Pope in Rome it was no big deal.

I couldn't believe I was actually thinking about doing this. I was a Jewish boy from North Jersey for Gods sake! I didn't know if churches had phones, and if they did, who would answer them? Mrs. B told me to look in her book for the priest's private number but all I could find was something called the rectory. I called the number but on this Sunday morning all I got was an answering machine. I found myself leaving a rather bizarre message asking them to hold up their Mass for the Mrs. Needless to say they didn't, and when she got home she pouted and I bore the brunt of her wrath later that Sunday. About five minutes before my shift was over I got the call.

"Brian," she called over the intercom in a singsong voice. "I am going to need a roast chicken tonight. The doggies are looking at me as if they need a special treat. Thank you." I hated those goddamned dogs.

Or how about the time she ranted and raved around the house because the Federal Drug Administration wouldn't let her super-special French facial cream through United States borders. You would think world peace was on the line or a police action was warranted by the way she was yelling and screaming on the phone to the state senator (an old friend of the family).

"I'm telling you, I want my cream!" she yelled over the phone to who I think was the senator's secretary. I guess after 20 minutes of Mrs. B's outrageousness, even an esteemed public servant like the state senator needed to pass the buck. After another 20 minutes of angry protest to this poor soul, the Mrs. finally hung up the phone.

"Brian, call the FDA and tell them I want that cream," she commanded.

Doesn't the supermarket have some facial products, I thought to myself before I carried out my unusual assignment? Again, I felt like the biggest idiot bowing to her crazy wishes but there I was, phone in hand. It took me about 2 hours before I could finally talk person to person with someone. I guess the FDA was busy wasting time making sure unsafe products weren't being brought into the country. Didn't they know that after some lengthy and mostly unbelieved explanation, Mrs. B's private chef was trying to wrangle some answers out of a low-level bureaucrat regarding the great face cream embargo of the 20th century? After all that time, the only option I was given was to clearly state my name, phone number, and concern into an answering machine and that I would be contacted on the matter at a later date. All that wasted time and energy, and to this day I still haven't heard another word about the elusive French face cream.

CHAPTER THIRTEEN

Some time during the next week I was informed by Francis, Michelle, and both B's, in writing, over the phone, and to my face that a large dinner party was being planned. The date had been set for the next Saturday evening, invitations were done by an expert calligrapher and were being hand-delivered by a limousine driven courier. The B's had invited some family members and other members of the city's royalty, a few of them heavy-duty food aficionados, including a world-famous chef and restaurateur. A well-known interior decorator was employed to oversee the lavish adornment of the already exquisite house with exotic flowers and ice sculptures. Members of the city's orchestra were going to be in the red room performing while their music would be piped throughout the house for all to enjoy. Food stations were going to be tastefully set up on the main grounds, including one of the most lavish and outlandishly expensive caviar set-ups this side of the Caspian Sea. A sommelier from a five star downtown restaurant would be pouring wines from the Mr.'s private cellar which I was told (by him) was the best on the East coast. All they needed was a piñata and some party hats and their gala would officially have everything.

"Brian," Mr. B had said to me. "The food had better be amazing, don't embarrass me." These words of encouragement are just what every employee likes to hear from his or her boss.

"Brian," Mrs. B would say to me through a cloud of cigarette smoke. "We really want to impress our guests this year. Do you want me to get you some help from the hotel?"

I took these words as a formal challenge. The gauntlet had been thrown down. "I think I may need a few people to help me plate up hors d' oeuvres and things like that the night of the party, but I am good to go until then," I said impressively. Unfortunately they had both left the kitchen before I finished my pronouncement and I realized I was only talking to a haze of cigarette smoke and the smell of scotch. God, I hated my job! I was going to give these people the best stuff I had and really knock them out with the food and presentation.

 I had a couple of hours before the dogs needed dinner so I decided to do some shopping for my party menu. Something was different about the produce section that day. Did they move the melons? Did they change the displays without notifying me? I asked myself. I wasn't quite sure, but I was sensing something awry. It was quiet in the produce section that day… too quiet. As I continued my perusal of the area looking for clues, I couldn't help but notice out of the corner of my eye a striking lady standing in front of the display of hot-house tomatoes. It took just one quick glance at this statuesque beauty for me to put my finger on the difference in that supermarket. Her features were exquisite—even the satiny, shiny, red skin of those lovely tomatoes couldn't stand up to that lady's seductively painted lips. She seemed so out of place standing there checking the firmness of those tomatoes; she would have been more believable in a fashion magazine like the ones Beth is always reading. Or maybe a high-budget porno movie! Yeah that's it, one where she is out looking for a good time in a supermarket… Wait, what the hell am I thinking? I am a married man, a *happily* married man. A happily married man with two kids… what were their names again?

 This woman was dressed to kill, with her thirty-something body displaying more bare, silky skin than those lucky, lucky tomatoes. I shook my head violently from side to side to try and snap myself out of it but instead found my cart steering over in her direction. The cart must have developed a mind of its own and I was powerless to change its desired destination. As I approached her, our eyes met and locked, causing my stomach to knot itself up tighter than Armenian string cheese. I quickly looked away, acting as if I needed some tomatoes even though they weren't on my list. Time seemed to stand still and we were both quite content living in that moment fondling the tomatoes. The closer I got to her, the more I could tell that she smelled good. The scent of her perfume was causing me to swoon. I think even the tomatoes were blushing. Accidentally, or so I first thought, her bare leg brushed up against mine. Shyly, I smiled and took a small step back.

"I don't bite ... hard," she softly informed me. "So, what's up with the sexy outfit?" she asked while looking me up and down.

I smiled at her but remained mute.

"Do you work for a restaurant around here or something?" she continued her questioning.

I had forgotten that I was wearing my chef's regalia.

"No, no, I don't work in a restaurant," I finally was able to say. I then paused for a second. I didn't want to sound pompous telling her I was a private chef. Most people tend to look at me strangely when I tell them that I personally cook for a family, so I said, "Actually I just cook for a couple people in the area."

"You're one of those private chefs, aren't you?" she blurted with admiration, showing much interest.

"Well, yes, that's my official title," I calmly replied, trying to play down the whole thing.

"Don't be so modest, I bet you can really cook ... can't you," she said with a sardonic grin, her body edging closer to mine. "A private chef, how fascinating, I sure wouldn't mind seeing you in my kitchen," she said, her eyes staring right into mine.

"It feels a little hot in here today ... don't you think?" I said nervously.

"I didn't notice," she said, edging even closer.

I could feel her hot breath on my neck, so I quickly turned away from her. My crotch area was becoming a bit uncomfortable, and I didn't want her to see, well, you know. She was slowly twirling a lock of her curly brown hair between her fingers, while her green eyes were batting her long black lashes.

"This private chef thing, is it a full-time job or do you have extra time for private cooking lessons?" she asked in a way I was totally unfamiliar with, but which I kind of liked. All of a sudden the unfortunate tomatoes, under which my hand was resting, gave way and caused me to awkwardly fall into the display and send tomatoes cascading down around our feet. She seemed to be enjoying how uncomfortable her game of seduction was making me. I was now perspiring heavily and I could also sense my face turning different shades of red. Slowly she bent down one knee in front of me, knowing full well her blouse was buttoned very low, giving me a full view of what her white, lacy bra was trying to contain. Being a gentleman, I bent down to help pick up the tomatoes but I couldn't stop staring at her aerobacized thighs as her already short skirt was riding high up her leg. She gazed directly into my eyes and I could tell that this lady was either very horny, hungry, or somewhere in between. All of a sudden she leaned towards me, her lips becoming bigger and fuller by the second. *My god*, I thought, *she is going to kiss me.* I was paralyzed with both delight and fear. Luckily, just before official contact was made, a stock boy arrived with broom in hand to sweep up any mess, along with any chances I might have had. I stood up quickly, feeling the sweat dripping down my back as I stepped away from the lady.

"Well, I better be getting back to my work," I said, feeling kind of relieved by the interruption.

"Leaving so soon? I'm not scaring you away, am I?" she said in a flirtatious purr.

"Ah, no, no, no," I stammered, stumbling on my denials. "I really have to get back to work, you know how it is," I commented with an official tone.

As I started to reluctantly move my cart away from hers, she said, "I hope to see you again sometime." With a wink and an alluring smile, she and all of her sculpted curves sauntered away, leaving me a little deflated but determined to get back to reality. I came to shop and shop I would, and then it was back to the house to finalize my menu for Mrs. B's approval.

The Last Nights of Spring
Hors D'oeuvres
Ivory Spoons of Foie Gras
Smoked Salmon on Corn Arepas
Crispy Turbot Wontons
Moroccan Cigars filled with Lobster
Warm Goat Cheese and Baby Peppers
Prosciutto Brie and Asparagus en croute
1st Course
Duck Consommé Star Anise Foie Gras Ravioli
2nd Course
Broiled Ricotta Gnocchi Coulis of Tomato White Truffle Oil
3rd Course
Curried Red Snapper Saffron Risotto Mango Chutney
4th Course
Roast Beef Tenderloin Roesti of Artichoke Port Wine Sauce
5th Course
Warm Chocolate Tart Praline Custard Coulis of Raspberry

CHAPTER FOURTEEN

Okay, this is it, I thought. The night to end all nights, the night that I was hoping would end in crowning achievement. The huge gala was upon me. After a week of intense shopping and prepping, my time to shine had come. My morning started unusually early. I woke up before Beth and the boys, and it was eerie not hearing the sound of cartoons echoing up to my bedroom from downstairs. I also finally caught Beth red-handed hogging all the covers and extra pillows on the bed… I knew it! The sun was just stretching its colorful fingers across the sky as I pulled into the near vacant Circle K for a hazelnut coffee and a donut. The highway felt as if it was mine alone; only a few big trucks were on the road along with a couple other early-morning toilers who were also forced to start their day with the night's sleep still lingering in their eyes.

I arrived at the B's for work at 6:00 A.M. With heavy-handed knocking I was able to awaken Josie, along with the dogs. Josie quickly came down to unlock the door wearing a powder-blue terry cloth robe and a pair of well-worn slippers. Her black curly hair that I had assumed to be her own was actually a wig, due to its cock-eyed position on her head. During her early-morning struggle to accommodate me she must have been too tired or too rushed to straighten it in the manner that kept her secret hidden, or maybe I was just the only one who never noticed. Needless to say, she scampered back upstairs as quickly as she came down them, leaving me alone with a couple of hungry dogs. Nothing like starting one of the most important days in your career with the preparation of an early morning snack for a couple of spoiled mutts.

I thought a few poached eggs and bacon should keep them quiet, and I was right. They slurped down their meal and went back upstairs to rest up for lunch. I on the other hand had work to do.

With the dogs out of my hair and the kitchen quiet and empty, I was able to concentrate on my finishing touches. Every detail, from hors d' oeuvre to dessert, needed to be perfect.

Precise quenelles of **foie gras** were studded with toasted almond slivers and black truffle, then sat gently in the miniature crevasses of delicate ivory spoons. Rosettes of thinly shaved smoked salmon were formed to adorn chive-laced corn **aerepas** for a la minute serving. A ginger and lime soy vinaigrette was emulsified for the dipping of turbot filled wontons. The Moroccan cigars, made with paper-thin phyllo dough, were filled with small chunks of Maine lobster, blanched fennel, and sautéed brunoise red pepper. Mini tri-colored bell peppers, cute as buttons, were stuffed with goat cheese and drizzled with lemon-infused olive oil and Japanese bread crumbs, then set aside, awaiting a hot oven to make the cheese warm and oozy. One-inch **roulades** of blanched asparagus tips, salty paper thin **prosciutto,** and creamy French brie were neatly rolled in puff pastry, egg washed and seasoned with kosher salt and crushed sesame seeds, then baked golden brown. All of these small treasures will later be lined soldier-like on small silver platters, paraded around a lavishly decorated patio by Francis and his fellow penguins. There they will meet their destiny by being admired for their looks and consumed for their flavor by fawning guests.

With all the hors d'oeurves completed, I was starting to feel a whole lot better. In most cases, these tiny bite-sized jewels can make up the most tenuous part of the entire meal preparation. They require an inordinate amount of attention. The proper completion and seasoning was vital to each one since they are, by nature, an individual bite. Plus, along with keeping the kitchen perpetually immaculate, making Mrs. B a quick lunch, doing a load of wash, refilling the sodas and waters, and having a fistfight with Francis, I needed to finish the rest of my work for the big dinner.

Oh, pardon me, did I just conveniently gloss over a juicy detail? Well, to begin with, Francis had a drinking problem. I couldn't say for sure if he was a full-fledge candidate for Alcoholics Anonymous, but Mothers Against Drunk Drivers certainly weren't giving any ringing endorsements to our tuxedoed friend. The word on the street (in other words, this came from Michelle) was that all too regularly, Francis was known for closing a bar or two around town. I didn't know why he drank so much, but you didn't need to be a rocket scientist to see that having his nose so far up the B's asses day after day had him so depressed that drowning his sorrows in a bottle of rum was the only way to ease his pain. Maybe his lack of family support or his grappling with his sexuality sent him running to the bars. Whatever the reason, his problems clearly needed a whole lot more attention than 2 am calls to the Psychic Hotline.

That morning wasn't the first time he slithered into work with bloodshot eyes and the smell of alcohol and Binaca on his breath. Come to think of it, it seemed that the night before any of the B's special occasions, when they either invited guests over or had a dinner party, he would get sloshed the night before. I noticed this a couple of times, but now my suspicions were confirmed. I remembered once when he caused me to screw up Grand Marnier soufflés by purposely lying to me about the time dessert was supposed to go out. I never could prove it, and of course he denied it, but in any case the soufflés came out of the oven a good 10 minutes too early and were embarrassingly flat by the time they were brought out to the dining room.

My wife feels that Francis's "foul moods" as she puts them were caused by his jealousy for not being the most important member of the crew. She thinks that because I was the chef, I received all the accolades (from the guests) on the special nights and that this must have really bothered him. Why else would he try to upset me or sabotage the meal? I guess she was probably right. Francis was a full-blown sycophant whose only moments of happiness were when the stick the B's made him fetch was thrown to him. But on these special nights, the B's tended to play a bit more fetch with me and that burned his balls. For whatever reason, I was walking on my own razor's edge that day and was not in any mood to take shit from him. The funny thing (funny weird, not funny ha-ha) about the whole altercation was that we had been on moderately good speaking terms for a couple of weeks. To many people, this wouldn't sound like the biggest example of friendship, but for us it was good progress. It wasn't even a week earlier we shared a chuckle about how he was only acting like half a dick instead of a whole dick the day of my car accident. Unfortunately, all of the building blocks to a good working relationship crashed down on both of us that particular day.

Francis arrived late and hung over that day, and I had already been a good three hours into my workday. I heard him scuffling around a bit in the laundry room, so I checked in on him to make sure he didn't disturb the prepped hors d'oeurves I put in there. Of course I caught him stuffing his face with some smoked salmon rosettes.

"What are you doing here so damn early?" He slurred his question while swallowing the salmon.

"I need to get ready for the party, remember? The dinner party the B's are having tonight?" I answered him, deciding to let the salmon incident pass without retort.

"Why try so hard, you'll just fuck it up anyway ... like that soufflé shit you made last time," he said, laughing to himself and walked towards the kitchen. I let him pass through without responding because I really did have a ton of work to do. In retrospect I should have nipped his pissy attitude in the bud.

A little while later I was still hard at work, Josie was downstairs helping Michelle get all the rooms ready for the party, and Mrs. B was flitting around the house, screwing up the flower arrangements the florist had spent hours on. Even Mr. B came home early from work to bring in some special white wines that he wanted to get properly chilled. I heard him yell for Francis to bring the wines down to the cellar as I left the kitchen to go to the herb garden for some fresh cuttings.

I was still fuming from Francis's earlier comments as I reentered the kitchen. I found him sitting at the kitchen island, that day's paper opened and half covering my cutting board and holding a cup of what I hoped was coffee in one hand.

"What's that smell, it smells like you're cooking a pot of shit," Francis commented, eloquently describing the aromas emitting from the port wine sauce. Even Josie and Michelle showed expressions of shock as they looked up from the silverware they were polishing. Before I could come up with the proper response, Michelle, surprisingly, stood up for me

"What's your problem? Don't tell me you're hung over again," she asked Francis, shaking her head in disgust.

Josie kept her head down, slowly shaking it from side to side. She knew not to get involved with employee bickering and never said a word.

"Mind your own business, bitch, I'm not talking to you," he snapped. "Besides, what the hell do you care about this asshole? You talk more shit about him than anyone else!" he reminded her, momentarily silencing her.

"Listen up!" she shouted, coming to her feet. "We all have our jobs to do today, and I think you should leave him alone to do his."

"Uh, don't you have some toilet bowls to scrub?" Francis asked sarcastically.

"Go to hell, you bleached blonde bastard!" she screamed her best response, almost in tears.

"Bleach your mustache, you stupid cow!" Francis retorted.

"Screw you!" said Michelle.

"Screw youuuuu!" Francis drawled.

Just as I was finally ready to cut in on the conversation, Mr. B burst into the kitchen, and all conversation quickly ended.

"Jesus Christ, Brian, I could hear your voice across the house," he boomed. "What in the hell is going on in here? If you think you are going to upset Mrs. B today, think again!"

I thought I was going to lose my temper! The Mr.'s berating me made me momentarily forget my hatred towards Francis. Fortunately, Francis would have none of that; he had the gall to agree with Mr. B.

"I don't know what his problem is, Brian started yelling at me as soon as I came in. He must be on his period or something, maybe he and Michelle are menstruating together," Francis said, obviously not forgetting about his fight with Michelle as he fell over himself to suck up. During this altercation, Josie was doing her best ostrich impression by keeping her head in the sand, only quickly lifting her eyes up long enough to pull good old Michelle down into the sand with her. Francis stood there with a satisfied expression on his face. Hatred was building inside of me as both of us waited for Mr. B's reaction. All I felt and saw was a look of utter disgust from Mr. B's face and it was mostly directed towards me. I was doing the best I could to just bite my lip and hold back my temper. I hadn't felt that powerless since I was a kid being reprimanded by the school principal for being naughty. But now I was no child, I was an adult, an adult getting his chain yanked none too gently. An adult whose back was up against the wall, being wrongly accused. I was sick of being laughed at, scorned and affronted. My anger bubbled up and exploded just like the fucking Grand Marnier soufflé Francis ruined weeks ago.

"THIS IS BULLSHIT, I HAVEN'T SAID ONE WORD! BUT I BET NOW YOU CAN HEAR ME ACROSS THE HOUSE!" I finally let loose my rage.

"Well then, what is going on in here? I tend to believe Francis, and he's told me how you like to cause trouble," Mr. B answered.

"Maybe if he could cook he wouldn't be such a nervous wreck about tonight's dinner," Francis added, once again with a bullshit chuckle.

"This is the last straw," I said, as serene and calm as I could be. It felt as if I entered into an out-of-body experience. I saw everything occur in slow motion. It felt like I was above the kitchen watching everything from above. Every sound and vision burst with clarity. Every fiber of my being felt free from abstractions or rules. I saw myself slowly walk over to Francis. I saw his jaw fluttering, his head moving forward and back like a bobblehead version of himself, his chuckles sounding odd in my obscure continuum.

I could see in great detail the tiny red veins in his bloodshot eyes. And I could feel the sinews of the muscles and tendons in my right arm cock itself back. I could feel the tight fist of my hand, and then see it hurl by and land squarely on Francis's skinny face.

Time and place, sound and vision, immediately returned to normal. Francis fell backwards about 15 feet. His flailing arms knocked over a few wineglasses, and the distinct sound of crashing glass drowned out the thud his limp body made as it landed on the hard kitchen floor. The girls immediately bent down to administer aid to Francis since a steady stream of blood was pouring from his nose. I guess I really got him good. The Mr. looked past Francis and then just shook his head at me, quite calmly in fact, and turned to leave the kitchen. He firmly informed me over his shoulder, now for the third time, not to screw up the dinner. He left the kitchen without even glancing at the bloody mess of his butler laying on the kitchen floor. He probably was more upset about the broken crystal wineglasses than anything else, now that I had time to think about it. Anyway, Josie helped Francis up and led him out of the kitchen and up the back stairs. Michelle went to the freezer to get some ice for his face. She gave me a disgusted look and told me I was wrong for hitting him. I said maybe it would help his hangover or something to that affect.

She just repeated, "That was wrong, that was wrong." She shook her head and left the kitchen.

So now she's Florence Nightingale? She's not even Florence Henderson! Of course, she was right, I really shouldn't have hit Francis, but I'd be lying if I said it didn't feel really, really good. Anyway, it probably wouldn't be the last time a chef was found going temporarily insane. This business has a tendency to do that to you, and that place, it would have driven Gandhi to violent madness.

Aside from the mess I made on Francis's face, the night was a smashing success. Imagine this large property on an absolute gem of an evening, lit up like a Christmas tree. The grounds possessed the aroma of a florist's shop as thousands of flowers perfumed the air. Rainbows of color could be seen dotting the flowing landscapes—rich purples, lavish pinks, brilliant reds, and pure whites, all the intense shades of the irises, crocuses, tulips and hyacinths (all planted by the Mexican gardener but overseen by the Mrs.).

Stretch limousines and $100,000 cars made their way through the opened iron gate and drove through this paradise up to the main entrance. Valets dressed in black tuxedos and stylish top hats opened car doors and escorted guests to the front door while footmen ran the cars to the back of the house. The guest's feet landed upon a red carpet and they followed it up the grand front door. The orchestra's melodic sounds were piped through the entire property; nowhere would a guest be without beautiful music. The female waiters carried goblets of the finest wines and champagnes to the incoming guests. An ice sculpture graced every room, but nothing was grander than the gigantic one in the red room that held in its crevices tin upon tin of the most expensive caviar in the world. Blini after blini were piled high with this fishy delicacy along with the appropriate garnishes of crème fraiche and lemon. Thousands of dollars were spent for these salty, plump fish eggs; unfairly, the Sturgeon saw nary a penny. The hors d'oeurves started pouring out of the kitchen with the mere flick of Mrs. B's diamond-encrusted wrist, as the ringing of her solid gold bell triggered the official start of the evening. Although I was tucked away in the kitchen, I overheard Francis and Michelle regaling tales of her sequined gown held up by her heavily jeweled hand so as not to touch the floor, cigarette in the other hand (I imagine she was afraid of gaining weight after the Japanese seamstresses practically sewed the gown onto her sticklike frame). She bypassed the Champagne and went immediately to her vodka on the rocks, which she sipped ever so carefully while giving her guests a full view of her amazingly sculpted profile. Mr. B. meanwhile was leaning next to the bar, where he started about four hours earlier, looking shlumpy in a tweed suit that had definitely seen better and thinner days. His only adornment was the copious amount of gold jewelry on his fingers and wrists, which tinkered against his highball glass again and again. They both did the required amount of mingling, the Mrs. raving about her upcoming trip to the Riviera and Mr. B boasting about breaking ground on his newest hotel.

The Mrs. led a few of the more special women through the rooms, casually pointing out priceless artifacts and striking *objets d'art* placed throughout the house. Both the Mr. and Mrs. seemed to relish these moments when all eyes were upon them. They lived to be the center of attention, to show off all their possessions of wealth, and to make it known to all that they lived the most pampered of lives. No expense was too costly for them; they would probably sell their souls for some acquisition their peer's held in high esteem. The height of success and excess was their only acceptable destination. These lavish galas helped cement their standing on the upward ladder of the most rich and famous.

For me, I was much more content being a behind-the-scenes player in this opulent extravaganza. My job performance would be evaluated within the boundaries of the gold-rimmed Russian plates that were once owned by some unnamed tsar. Possibly one of the Alexanders or

Katherines enjoyed a grilled cheese or a B.L.T. on one of these plates. It didn't matter who left their historic crumbs on those irreplaceable platters, it was in my hands to prepare the meal that would provide a new set of crumbs.

The flow of the meal, a most underrated part, went superbly. The Mrs. had a knack at timing each course. She was able to balance the time the sommelier needed to pour the appropriate wine with the time I needed to plate up the food. She was a magician, and her gold bell was her wand. She conducted the dinner as a maestro would a concert, all without missing the gist of a conversation or flicking off the ashes of her burning cigarette. Everyone had a part to play in her bacchanal: the Mr. foots the bill, the Mrs. looks the part, the waiters serve, the bartenders pour, the valets park, and last, but arrogantly far from least, was me, the chef.

The chef is the esteemed filler of the belly. He serves his calling by tempting the guests with sumptuous gastronomic fare. He could be either applauded or cursed, while he tries to send taste buds dancing with his epicurean delights, at the same time making waistlines expand to uncomfortable proportions. The ladies of the crowd, perhaps, have the toughest challenge—their snug gowns, already stretched to capacity, may not be able to afford even one too many calories. Half of these women must succumb to bulimia in order to maintain their waiflike figures. I couldn't imagine all my hard work being thrown up into the immaculate bowls of the B's bathrooms moments after being consumed, but I figured that comes with this bizarre territory.

The meal could have quite possibly been the finest of my career. Every ingredient I used was both the freshest available and of the highest quality money could buy. The duck consommé, strategically siphoned from under its porous **raft**, came out crystal clear, and the plump ravioli garnish, full of foie gras and truffle, floated in the bath of flavorful broth. The next course, a single ricotta cheese gnocchi, sat in a small pool of tomato coulis where not even the slightest hint of pressure would send the fork straight through these feather-light creations. Crispy skinned red snapper filet, hinted with flavors of spicy curry and sweet mango, was so powerful that one taste sent you flying on a magic carpet ride of satisfaction. Kobe beef tenderloin, so tender, so sublime, was cooked to a perfect medium-rare. The meat's pink flesh was neatly shingled on a rustic artichoke and potato **roesti**, the inherent juices of the meat married perfectly with the port wine sauce. Finally, the warm chocolate tarts, hiding their decadent liquid elixir inside their warm and firm cake shell, were positioned on a plate painted with streaks of raspberry sauce and crème anglaise.

This was a meal for the modern day kings and queens of high society. Millionaires and billionaires alike were treated as equals on this special occasion, and the B's accepted their complements as desolate desert dwellers accept water. "Keep it coming," I imagined was the chorus that reiterated in their minds after each course.

I did my job, despite the extracurricular events of the day, and left with a feeling of accomplishment and achievement. No, of course, the B's didn't bring me out in front of their guests for a bow or applause. I never received any compliments the whole evening, unless you call Francis and Michelle eating leftovers off the plates they brought back into the kitchen an endorsement. I did, however, receive a nod of assent from Mr. B after dessert when I was cleaning up. He poked his head into the kitchen, his face beet red (he looked like Rudolph the disgustingly rich and drunk reindeer). He probably polished off at least one bottle of Scotch by this time. He looked at me, I'm not sure for how long… I guess he was just waiting for me to look in his general direction and when I did, I got my thanks, a nod, and then back to his guests he returned. The food stains on his shirt and on his face were the only proof that he actually liked the dinner.

After a meal of this magnitude, the clean up was horrendous. Thank

God Michelle and Francis had the foresight to get extra help from the hotel. Extra servers and dishwashers made the potentially hellish night actually not so bad. I had my kitchen back in order by the time the men had retired to the library with cigars and brandy and the women were puking it up in the bathroom. By that point I was so done with that place and I had only a few things on my mind: getting out of that house, smoking a cigarette, and getting home for a well-deserved beer. Without even speaking to the slightly swelled Francis or the exhausted Michelle and Josie, I did just that.

CHAPTER FIFTEEN

Spring naturally leads into summer, and this year was no different. The temperatures were rising, the days were getting longer, and the B's annual excursion to the South of France was right around the corner. Mrs. B was busy packing up her crates of necessities (or should I say having everyone else do it) for her summer of roughing it in yet another paradise. I was constantly being sent to store after store for things she couldn't possibly live without on her ten-acre villa in Provence. I guess even in Europe she couldn't get over herself.

Aside from that, things had been going all right, especially considering the circumstances. The B's and I continued to have a relationship no greater than minor acquaintances would share. It was a rare occurrence for them to even moderately acknowledge my presence, let alone actually give me a respectable greeting despite me working in plain sight every day in their kitchen. My feelings at that point were more along the lines of an "I could care less" attitude—if they wanted to treat me like an invisible servant then so be it.

Obviously, the thought of me accidentally seasoning their **pasta Bolognese** with rat poison had never crept into their minds, although I must admit I had spent a few tranquil moments relishing the possibility of their rich bodies convulsing on their freshly waxed atrium floor. Oh yes, I could see it all too well, their cold blood turning colder, their complexions turning ashy as they clutched at their throats, their eyes showing that they finally knew they had pushed me a little too far when they had me make and decorate birthday cakes for their stupid dogs. I also got the extra bonus thought of there being lots of vomit for Francis to clean up.

Or I would fantasize about hurting the B's where it really counted. For people like them there are things worse than death, and it wouldn't be too hard for me to play the role of a modern-day Robin Hood. A little embezzling here, a little thievery there. How sweet the notion was of adding to my molehill by subtracting from their mountain. Of course, these were just dreams, and more importantly, they are serious crimes, ones I certainly wasn't prepared to pay for.

As far as the rest of the gang went, I had managed to alienate myself from everyone in the slave-pool. Ever since I punched Francis in the face the night of the party, he hadn't spoken one word to me, nor had anyone else. I didn't know if it was a coincidence or not but even the gardeners were giving me attitude when I walked through the gardens. As an added bonus, Michelle taught Francis the communication technique of written correspondence, so now I got his and her notes, along with Mrs. B's notes. Some mornings I have an entire book waiting for me on my workstation. It would have been sad if I hadn't gotten so many laughs reading their stupid notes with their atrocious spelling and even worse grammar.

All the running around for the B's trip was putting a strain on everyone. Michelle and Francis were barely civil to me but they were even worse to each other. They even began leaving notes for each other rather than speaking, and every morning my cutting board was littered with their correspondence. No matter how I pleaded with or screamed at them, they couldn't figure out that I hated their shit on my work area. It was one more indignity I was forced to live with in this hellhole. It was depressing because in my other life I never would have allowed half the stuff I was forced to endure at the B's.

I didn't need a Tarot card reader to tell me that there was no future for me here. I'd given this place my best effort and clearly it wasn't enough. I tried not to let it bother me that I spent most of my week with a group of people who hated my guts. I mean, it was not easy being the central point in a circle of loathing from a couple of morons and some rich people who thought I was no better than dirt. All I wanted to do was be creative and prepare good food in peace, but because I wanted to preserve a tiny bit of self esteem and not kiss ass all day, I was the black sheep of the house. I was training myself to care less and less; my wife thought it was the only way for me to stay sane. And that was not an easy thing to do when you didn't get any positive feedback from people you cooked for.

By this point, Beth thought I was nuts to keep working for the B's. She said it was pathetic how I hadn't received a raise or bonus or even a sincere thank you after all the hard work I'd done, including the home run I hit at the last dinner party. She was probably right, but before the B's vacation there was only one small brunch for the Sotheby's people and then they were off to France for 6 whole weeks. I figured I could collect a check every week, have very little stress, and try to enjoy my time without them. Maybe after the summer I would make a move, but I'd bide my time until then.

I had been told that once every year, the Sotheby Company sent a few representatives out to the B's mansion for a small lunch and appraising session. Mrs. B had it all figured out—the meal would be a simple one, and she told me it would "help the situation" (which meant it would butter up the evaluators). Mrs. B had a theory that since the representatives were, in her words, "gay players," the best way to their stomachs and calculators would be with a healthy wedge of quiche. I doubt any gay and lesbian alliances would be condoning this thought process any time soon.

She certainly had a way of giving new meaning to both stereotyping and stupidity. Is was her idiotic ideas like these that gave ultimate proof that she was definitely the bread spender and not the bread earner of this family. Would anyone in their right mind think that any homosexual would be so weak, gullible, and naïve that they would risk both career and integrity for a freaking piece of quiche? I could see maybe bribing them with, say, maybe money! "Hello! … Earth to Mrs. B, they are gay, not poor and starved rats." I was pretty sure these men were highly paid professionals who I think could come up with a few dollars of pocket change for some baked eggs in a pie crust. Good Lord, I shudder to think what she would have had me prepare for a couple of lesbians. As it turned out, the appraisers who ended up coming were 2 middle-aged men and 1 middle-aged woman, none of which held any sexual connotations for, nor biases toward, quiches, flans, frittatas, or baked egg products of any kind. They just came alone with nothing but honest assessments of the B's valuables. Just another interesting day in the bowels of the unfeeling monster that was life in this rich bitch's presence.

CHAPTER SIXTEEN

The B's summer vacation was finally here. The whispers of the prodigal son's arrival, coupled with their trip to France, were causing quite a stir within the household. The B's were happily anticipating the homecoming of their only son and then they would be off on their private jet, taking them across the Atlantic. As for the help, they had the massive job of packing the B's for their trip. I was dumbfounded by the amount of crap they took. Mrs. B filled three suitcases herself with just shoes! Hell, a pair of sandals and a pair of sneakers and I'm easily a go for the whole summer. But I guess her grand total of 39 bags would just have to suffice (39 designer bags, that is). Thirty-nine bags it took to ensure that she could be amply clothed for a 6-week trip. Didn't they have washing machines in France? Plus they go there every year… wouldn't you think she had some kind of wardrobe waiting for her over there? Evidently not. My god, If I took every article of clothing my entire family owned, from my wife's g-strings to my kids' winter gloves, I don't think I could fill more than a quarter of the amount of bags this crazy broad took.

As for the excitement surrounding their son's arrival… well, I didn't know much about him. I'd only had a few small conversations with Josie that shed some light on the subject. Apparently, their parent–son relationship wasn't one that was taken from the pages of Little House on the Prairie. It was more like "rich white boy raised by his black nanny and ignored by his socialite parents in the big house on the prairie."

His name was Andrew, named after Mr.'s deceased father, and he was the Mr.'s second child… the other one from his first marriage I hadn't met yet. Both his first-born child and his first wife were taboo subjects and were seldom brought up by anyone in the house. Mrs. B had all but erased any traces of the Mr.'s first life, like any good trophy wife would do. There was not one piece of evidence in any of the rooms I'd been in to prove they even existed. I learned most of my information on them from a couple of boxes I found deep in the basement one day when I was on some wild goose chase for Michelle. There were all sorts of pictures and souvenirs of his previous life banished from the light of day. The Mr. looked a lot different in the old days, he actually seemed happier and certainly a lot thinner. His ex wife was not all that attractive but it wasn't a long shot in guessing that her temperament and demeanor were a lot more amicable than the new Mrs. B. The story on the hows and whys of the divorce are unknown to me, but if I had to speculate, I would assume the new Mrs. B had more than a little to do with the breakup. She was a scheming one all right. Unlike Eve in the Garden of Eden, she needed no serpent to assist in her plans, and just like Adam, Mr. probably had no choice but to succumb to temptation. He took the Mrs.'s bait hook, line, and sinker. The rest was history, the Mrs. was now the matriarch of this vast estate and fortune, and having a child was simply either for kicks or for inheritance purposes.

This Andrew, except for his little trip through his mother's birth canal, was the closest thing to a bastard, without actually being one, as someone could get. I heard that right after he was born he was immediately handed over to Josie's possession, and Josie's small wing of the house became no more than an orphanage for young Andrew. While the B's went gallivanting from country to country, living the lives of the rich and famous, the little boy slowly grew up under Josie's capable care. It was Josie who stayed up to all hours rocking him to sleep when he was fussy. It was Josie who potty trained him, fed him, bathed him, and ultimately loved him. Josie taught him to crawl, then walk, then run, and run he did, from boarding school to boarding school, then eventually to private high schools and finally college. It's no wonder he choose to go to a college outside the United States border, and then only to come home no more than once a year.

Of course now, the B's were making a big deal about his returning home, telling everyone that everything must be just so for the little Lord of the Manor. Around the staff, the Mrs. is known for her seething jealousy toward Josie because of all the attention Andrew gives to her, even though she has nobody to blame but herself. She handed the boy off to her the minute she got home from the hospital and never looked back. Sometimes when a letter arrived for Josie from Andrew, Mrs. B would take her anger out on Josie by adding further work for her to do around the house. Mrs. B had been known to conveniently find messes for Josie to clean right when Josie sat down to eat or was ready to retire for the evening. Rooms that nobody had been in for months suddenly needed cleaning. Mrs. B sure wasn't the queen of subtlety.

The B's must have skipped a whole generation of music. Little did they know a band called The Beatles once sang "Money can't buy you love," and now the B's were finding that to be true with Andrew. Their idea of parenting consisted of refilling his bank account every month, allow him unlimited credit card usage, and throwing other monetary presents his way. This form of child rearing was not quite the mantra Dr. Phil uses. Hell, Dr. Spock, Dr. Dolittle, and Dr. Detroit for that matter wouldn't condone such a practice. This concept had done nothing more than create a wealthy vagabond who had never finished a single school year in the same school he started. So, really, it wasn't much of a surprise when Andrew told his parents that he would rather not go on vacation with them, and that instead he wanted to spend two weeks home and then fly back to England. This did not sit well with the B's as was overheard by all of us during their not-too-pleasant-sounding phone calls leading up to his arrival.

Raised voices, resentment, and hard truths all were featured in the daily sessions over the phone the three days preceding his flight home. But it didn't seem like a deep emotional pain like any normal parent would feel. My slant on the whole situation was that the B's didn't seem upset that their only son shunned the idea of spending time with them in France; it was anger of a narcissistic nature. Andrew was possibly the only person in the world who didn't bow down to their every want and need. The B's were in the business of owning humans as if they were mere possessions, but in Andrew's case they had someone who didn't wear a price tag. So, like any paranoid, egotistical, passive-aggressive personalities would do, the B's rationalized a lame excuse for his unwillingness to accompany them to France.

"Our son, Andrew, had a grueling year at school, so him and a couple of his friends are going to relax for a couple of weeks around the pool," Mr. B told me one afternoon.

Mrs. B told a similar story. "I want you to provide him with anything he needs. My poor boy has worked so hard at school, and he needs to take it easy," she commanded us, stressing the word "anything." I hated that kid already.

Andrew arrived from the airport in a white limousine. Francis went out to assist the driver with the bags. I guess he never learned his mother's packing technique. At first impression he seemed to me like an average 21-year-old kid. He wore the mandatory Walkman on his head, a simple white shirt, blue jeans, and sneakers. Nothing extravagant, nothing flashy, no cry for attention. He just resembled an average kid returning home from college.

He was a refreshing surprise, I honestly was expecting a spoiled brat. I would have had to been deaf not to hear all of Francis's and Michelle's complaining since the B's announcement that he was staying at the house that summer. They seemed to perpetuate the image of him being a whining, sniveling pain in the ass. In some ways Francis and Michelle sounded as if they were too good to wait and serve just Andrew. As if it would be slumming it to serve such an unworthy subject, one who wouldn't be swayed by their brown nosing. My motto was more simplistic in nature: he had a mouth and it was connected to his stomach, and therefore I would feed him. What other reason was I there for? I wondered if I would be doing any shopping for him? If he had any of his mother's gall or lack of humility, then he would be sending me to the store for condoms, jock itch powder, and pornos.

Instead of a conceited and spoiled rich kid, I met a nice, well-mannered guy. He was about 6 feet tall and had brown, semi-spiky hair and wore a trusting smile. He introduced himself with a handshake and a hello. The possibility of me having a contagious disease that only impoverished servants carry never seemed to have crossed his mind. He introduced himself as Andrew, although he knew I knew his name and I told him mine. Pleasantly he asked if he could have a couple cookies, and I was really in shock. He didn't seem to care that I pretty much worked for him, he just had nice manners.

"There is milk in the fridge," I told him. What else could I say? The reality was he didn't have to ask for a thing, in a sense he was part owner of everything in this entire house, and that included a couple of stupid cookies.

"A Sprite's cool," he said. He grabbed a can to go along with his cookies and upstairs he went.

I had a real good feeling about this kid; he seemed nothing like his parents and instead seemed really cool, I thought that the summer might not suck as much as I feared.

"Where's Andrew?" Mrs. shouted at me as she barged into the kitchen.

"He went upstairs, I think," I replied.

"He didn't come in to see me… what did you say to him?" she practically barked, as if I were to blame for her son's lackluster greeting.

"I said … 'Hi'. Was that wrong?" I asked with a hint of sarcasm.

"Ugh!" she shouted, and off she went.

That was the most fun I had ever had in her kitchen.

CHAPTER SEVENTEEN

The following morning the B's were off to France in a haze of cigarette smoke and perfume. I thought they would never leave with all the last minute instructions they were leaving for Andrew and the Dogs. Or maybe I should say the Dogs and Andrew: I wouldn't want to fool you into thinking that they actually gave more thought to their only son that to those two fucking animals.

After their departure, so went my daily culinary challenges. Andrew only requested the simplest things to eat. He usually sat in the kitchen with me while I cooked and we talked, and he certainly was a talker. We actually had a few very interesting conversations. The subjects mostly revolved around philosophy, music, and politics. Once, while I was re-cleaning the already clean kitchen, we found that we had very similar tastes in music and he turned me on to some bands that I still listen to even today. He told me he wasn't sure what he wanted to do with his life and that he was evolving up at college, taking all different kinds of classes. He was a smart, down-to-earth kid who was looking for a career that would interest him. He changed his major almost every semester since starting at his university, looking for something that would best suit him. Apparently, all the money in the world couldn't make the quest to find his calling any easier. From that point forward, I almost believed that the next two weeks would work out just fine. Except for the few times I spoke with Mrs. B's secretary, I rarely had a person in that house with whom I could enjoy a conversation

It didn't take very long for Francis and Michelle to take notice of the large amounts of time that Andrew was spending in the kitchen. They also discovered him doing the unimaginable (such as eating with me in the kitchen instead of in one of the more acceptable dining rooms). To them it was like Donald Trump standing at a counter scarfing down White Castle burgers instead of sitting in a glamorous restaurant in Manhattan. I could tell they did not like how this summer was going at all. They were so used to having Mrs. B around throwing crumbs of affection at them that the Brian/Andrew friendship was freaking them out.

They tried to give me the silent treatment, but the problem was, those idiots didn't seem to realize I *loved* not having to talk to them. Secondly, it wasn't producing the right result, which was me quitting the job so they could get a new chef in there to torment. Maybe they were pissed because the old chef got the job of interviewing new chef candidates while their two cents went completely unheeded. I think they wanted to be the ones to choose the next chef, one who would understand the pecking order that they invented, with the chef at the bottom of the pole.

I wondered who would break first and speak to me, and my first guess was right. It was Francis. He came up to me one morning, after spending the night in the Mr.'s study, drinking his scotch and smoking his cigars, and he casually began a conversation with me.

"You know, if you want, you can, you know, have your wife, uh, come to the house and, uh, kind of, you know, give her a tour or something," Francis said.

I stared into his bloodshot eyes, not trusting a single word that came out of his mouth.

"Maybe," I shrugged, not giving any hint that I noticed that these were the first words he had spoken to me in weeks.

"Oh," he said, and not knowing what else to do, he shuffled back to the study to continue where he'd left off last night.

Francis was so transparent. I knew that if I took him up on his offer it would be used against me when the B's got home. Mrs. B had a strict rule against any of the staff having people at her house. Francis was such an asshole. Even though he had friends in and out most mornings, I never even thought of it as a possibility. Plus, there was no way I would want Beth to ever come to that house and meet those two knuckleheads; it was too depressing to even think about.

From then on, Francis and Michelle were constantly following me, trying to catch me break any of the Mrs.'s rules. I saw the predatory look in their eyes, even when they were faking being nice to me. They wanted some ammunition by the time the B's got home from Europe. Their jealousy over my strengthening friendship with Andrew was eating them up, and I don't think they cared about anything else except being important to this creepy family. The thing was, I couldn't have cared less about what they were trying to do. I didn't to do anything out of the ordinary, I just did my work as always and whatever happened, happened.

After a couple of days without the B's, I was running out of things to do. The bulk of my responsibilities didn't take six weeks to finish; maybe one week would have been a lot more realistic. My duties basically pertained to any object, appliance, or area that remotely fell under the headline of "kitchen." This included scrubbing trash cans, cleaning the grill, polishing the copper pots and pans, sharpening every piece of cutlery on the premises, and replacing the shelf paper in the pantry. There was no need for me to rush to get out of work early because the Mrs. had a way of checking in on us at all hours of the day. It was just last week that she docked one of the gardener's pay because he wasn't at work when she called. Even though the Mrs. called 5 minutes before the end of his shift, the house still received a fax from France outlining her displeasure and documenting his wage garnishment. Like a true jerk, Francis left the fax on the kitchen island for a couple hours before bringing it out to him, where I couldn't help but read it. I hadn't even finished it before I realized that I didn't want to receive one like it.

Michelle, Francis, and Josie didn't seem to be having any problems keeping busy, at least appearing busy, so a letter like this wasn't going to pose much of a threat. They had the luxury of being permitted to venture through the entire house where no room, hallway, or staircase was off limits. Which is to say, they were able to hide their lying around doing nothing from the schmuck stuck in the kitchen.

Josie, who had her own room, spent most of her time in it watching daytime television. She had her eyes glued to everything from Jerry Springer to Oprah. She was obsessed with those wild talk show scenarios. She basically shuttled tins of sardines and Diet Cokes up to her room and held herself hostage there. She would occasionally come out of her self-imposed exile to spend time with Andrew. I watched them through the back door as they would take the long way around the house to get to the pool. Josie never had any intention to swim, but it gave her a chance to converse in peace with her adopted son. Andrew, as any gentleman or a good son would, showed real surprise when Josie would decide not to swim when they reached the pool's edge. She would sit on one of the immaculate and upholstered lounge chairs for a time while he would swim and enjoy the sun and eventually she would leave him there and stroll happily back to the house and to her television.

As for Francis and Michelle, they were living in some sort of warped reality. They hadn't gone so far as calling themselves Mr. and Mrs. B, but they were certainly acting as if they were them. Francis found himself quite at home sitting in Mr.'s favorite chair in the living room, puffing on the Mrs.'s cigarettes or lounging in the TV room with a glass of Scotch in hand, stuffing his face with $12 a pound cashews. Michelle's ever-fattening ass was a few chairs away, her bare feet up on the antique coffee table, reading the Mrs.'s fashion magazines, imagining herself wearing the impossibly expensive clothes and accessories. On this day, she was too tied up with an article to acknowledge my presence when I went down to tell them of my plans for Andrew's party.

CHAPTER EIGHTEEN

Andrew informed me, soon after his parents' departure, that a couple of his friends were flying in from London and that he wanted to have a pizza party for them on Friday night. From a culinary standpoint I was excited because he had only eaten the simplest of dishes: macaroni and cheese, burgers, chicken tenders, the same stuff my kids eat. Also, pizza is one of my favorite things to make… the fresh yeast, the warm dough, the smell of the garlic and tomato from the homemade sauce always had a way of making me happy.

"I'm just here to inform you what I need for the party tonight," I said that day to the two other servants. There was no reaction. Michelle kept reading and Francis started scrolling through the thousands of cable channels.

"I know you can hear me, but understanding me, well that's another story." I continued. When they looked up I grinned. "Ah, now I have your attention."

"What are you doing down here? You know you're not allowed in this part of the house," Francis snapped. "Besides, Andrew is your buddy, you take care of it."

"Look, it's your job to serve, it's my job to cook," I answered.

No comment followed. At this point, I wish I'd thought ahead and brought a camera with me to capture the way these two morons really spent their time. Instead, Francis went back to his nuts, while Michelle turned another page of her magazine. I could see it was useless to ask for help from them and asking Josie to serve the food wasn't fair either. Instead, I decided to pre-cook all the pizzas and leave Andrew directions, explaining how to finish them. I was also adept enough to set up a little buffet with plates, napkins, and any other odd or end they would need to enjoy their party.

Thin crust pizzas
Homemade brownies

The thin crust pizza was one of my favorite things to make. These hand-crafted circular treats surpassed any take-out pizza. There are no secrets to making a good pizza; just use fresh ingredients, make your own dough, and get a really good pizza stone.

This dough is best made in a 5-quart mixer with a dough-hook attachment.

1 warm cup of water + 2 tablespoons
3/4 package of active dry yeast
Splash of olive oil
Pinch of Kosher salt
3 cups of all-purpose flour

1. Mix 2T of warm water with yeast in mixing bowl with a whisk.
2. Put mixing bowl on machine and add olive oil and the rest of the water.
3. Turn mixer to a low speed and add the flour and salt.
4. Let mix on slow until flour is slightly incorporated.
5. Turn mixture to medium-high at let run until the dough forms a ball and adheres to the dough hook and not the mixing bowl.
6. Let the dough **knead** for a minute on a medium-low speed.
7. Take dough out of mixing bowl, then lightly oil bowl and place dough back in the bowl. Cover with Saran wrap and place in a warm place to **proof**.
8. When the dough is doubled in volume, take out and place on floured surface.

9. Cut into 4 equal pieces and slightly kneed and roll each piece into a ball.
10. Once again cover the dough and let rest for about 15-20 minutes.
11. Roll out the dough, one at a time, with a rolling pin on a floured surface as thin as you can.
12. Roll dough on rolling pin to pick up easier and lay on a super-hot pizza stone that has been lightly dusted with cornmeal.
13. Quickly add your sauce, cheese, and toppings and get it back in the oven.
14. Bake until the bottom of the crust is a rustic-brown and the cheese is a yummy-bubbly.
15. With a pizza **peel**, remove the pie and place on a cutting surface.
16. Cut and enjoy.

Toppings for pizza can greatly vary. In this case, I kept it simple but stressed quality ingredients. The sauce was freshly made with skinned and seeded diced plum tomatoes sautéed with olive oil, garlic, and fresh basil. A touch of canned tomato puree and chicken stock stretched the sauce and also helped bring it together. The cheeses were a combination of fresh mozzarella, grated mozzarella, parmesan, and a dry ricotta. For toppings, I used fresh basil leaves, thin slices of prosciutto, minced capers, and kalamata olives. Simple but divine.

Friday morning arrived and with it an absolutely gorgeous summer day. Andrew's friends flew in from London the night before. He told me he was going to meet them in the city for drinks and they would get home very late. I spent my morning making the pizzas and re-shelf papering the pantry shelves.

At four o'clock the kids were still sleeping. I know it sounds weird to call a group of 21 year olds kids but that's how I thought of them. I pre-baked 4 pizzas and left them on pie plates on the kitchen island with instructions for heating them. The pizzas looked very tempting, and the smell alone was making me hungry. I knew all too well the sensual pleasure I get when my mouth bites down on this crispy crusted, cheesy, Italian/American fare.

Technically my day was over, but unfortunately, I still had an hour or so to go until my official quitting time. I knew that I couldn't count on Francis or Michelle to cover for me if the Mrs. called and that I would have to wait it out, so I went out to the servant's porch to smoke a cigarette. I was surprised to find it occupied by two English girls. They introduced themselves as Sharon and Tracy. Sharon seemed to be over 6 feet tall, with an exotic mane of red hair that fell to the middle of her ass. She had gorgeous green eyes and a scattering of freckles across her nose and shoulders. She was wearing a white tank top without a bra, and a pair of cut-off navy blue sweat pants. Tracy, her younger sister, was also tall, but a curly haired brunette with well toned legs and a fire-breathing dragon tattoo on the small of her back (um, not that I was looking or anything).

They both seemed to perk up considerably in my presence. Girls at that age must be happy to see any older man, because I figured I must have been at least fifteen years older than them. Also, my dirty chef uniform wasn't the most attractive thing in the world, so maybe they were bored. We engaged in small talk for a few minutes. I told them that I was the house chef, they told me that they were friends with Andrew at college.

"Andrew said there was a pool," the redhead said. "Maybe you could show us where it is?"

I figured there would be no harm in accommodating a guest. Besides, I had the time.

"This way. It's not too far," I said as I led them through the grounds.

I was starting to feel a bit self-conscious because they were giggling to each other only a few feet behind me, stopping each time I turned back to check on them. Once we reached the pool, however, the giggling stopped.

"Oh my lord, this is gigantic," said Tracy as she walked around the stunning pool's enormous perimeter.

"I want to go in, can I?" Sharon asked me, not being aware that I wasn't even allowed up here, let alone out of my jurisdiction of the kitchen.

"Well, Sharon… your name's Sharon, right?" I asked, stalling. "The thing is, it's just that, you know, maybe Andrew can a … ah … oh my God," I almost screamed, for there in front of me was a tattooed English girl swimming naked in the B's pool and…. Oh Jesus, make that two naked English girls swimming naked in the B's pool.

"Come on in, the water feels great," Sharon beckoned to me, her sister nodding as well. The only thing I could think to do was pretend that I didn't hear or see them.

"Come on, get in here," Sharon yelled again.

"Well, I would, but, uh, its just that I'm not really allowed in the pool since I'm a worker and all," I reluctantly explained. The fact that I was married also played in my mind.

"Go wake up Andrew, I'm sure he will let you in," Tracy chimed in.

"An excellent idea, I commend you on your choice, I will go see Andrew," I said as I quickly left the set of "English girls gone wild."

I went back to the house with every intention of changing my clothes and going home. I did not want to take another trip to temptation island. However, when I got back to the kitchen I saw that the rest of the late sleepers were up and looking for food. Andrew introduced the other two guests, a girl named Megan and a guy named Clive. All four of them went to school in London with Andrew. Andrew laughed when he told me that all of his friends' first-class airline tickets were being charged on his father's American Express Card, and I had to laugh at that as well. Two minutes later, everyone was into the brownies already and all had some sort of alcoholic beverage by their sides.

"Where's Francis, is he around?" Andrew asked me with a mouthful of brownie. "I want him to take my car in for a tune-up."

"Oh, I'm sure he's working real hard somewhere," I said sarcastically.

"Brian doesn't like Francis," Andrew said to his guests.

"No, no, I like him, it's just that…" I started, but I was interrupted before I could think of what to say.

"You can't stand him, I can tell," Andrew stated.

"Who's this Francis dude? He sounds real proper and all?" asked Clive.

"He is my parent's butler, they love him… probably more than me," Andrew replied, his eyes looking down at the counter. Actually hearing him say the words gave me chills up my spine.

"Hey, Brian, what are your plans tonight?" Andrew inquired.

"My plans? Well, I really don't have any except…" Once again I was cut off by his youthful excitement.

"Great, you have to hang out a bit, my man Clive has got some killer stuff," he said with undaunted enthusiasm.

"Yo, Brian, dude, you're gonna love this stuff, this is the shit," Clive said, nodding his head at me as he inhaled deeply from the bag he was holding.

"Brian, have you seen the other girls?" Megan asked me, for some reason grabbing my arm.

"They are at the pool, I'm pretty sure," I told her.

"Oh, come show me, will you please," she said, pulling me toward the door.

"Bring her up there, Bri, and turn on the hot tub for me, will ya?" asked Andrew.

"Hot tub! Come on, let's go!" Megan yelled, pulling me out the door as fast as she could, and off we were up to the pool. She certainly was spry.

Megan must have heard the other girls hooting and hollering because she proceeded to make a mad dash toward their voices. She was the prettiest of the three girls and the way she was hanging all over Andrew in the kitchen, I figured they were a couple.

The whole group of them seemed all right, but I couldn't help but wonder if they hung out with Andrew for his personality or his money. I never really had any friends of his financial magnitude, not now or ever, so I didn't have any personal experience with having friends with money. In this case, I really didn't get the impression that they were of the gold-digging variety, and during my tenure here, I certainly saw my share of people like that. I hoped that in their reality, they were just a tight circle of friends enjoying a couple of days together.

By the time we got to the pool area, the cabana's bar was raided, the stereo was turned on, and the hot tub was bubbling away. Tracy was mixing up a concoction of some sorts, and was polite enough to offer me one. I respectfully declined just as Andrew and Clive came up behind me to join the party.

"You must have one of her drinks, they are tops," said Clive.

"Just pour him one, and give it to him, don't ask, it's a party," said Andrew, grinning at me.

Tracy handed me a big glass of something and asked why I was still dressed.

"Why don't you come join us in the spa," Megan said as she turned away to join with the other girls. Her bare bottom had a small birthmark on the right, very perky cheek. I took a couple of sips of my drink (for quality control purposes, I assure you) and found that it wasn't half bad. In fact, it was damn good. Meanwhile, Andrew and Clive slipped into some bathing suits (thank God) and went for a dip in the pool.

I stood and stared out at the pool for a minute, feeling not quite right all of a sudden. Andrew gave me one of his bathing suits and told me to get into the hot tub. Who was I to argue with the boss's son? The bathing suit was a tad small for me and I was feeling a little self-conscious in it. Pretty soon though, as I moved closer to the hot tub, those feelings began slipping away. Even my extreme wedgie was all but forgotten, and I felt totally perfect. In fact, everything *was* perfect; the day, the night, the whole world was just totally cool. It was if I had been beamed into another dimension. I could see the imperfections on the shell of my soul, and I could reach out and pluck them off, one by one.

    The three English beauties rose from the steamy hot tub and walked over to me in a slow-motion sort of way. Their beautiful, sexy, wet bodies were dripping in the reflections of the sun. Swollen drops of water crashed to the ground, sending minute insects running for cover. Sharon took my glass for a refill and Tracy took my hand and led me back to the hot tub. We sat in the large cauldron of hot liquid, steam swirling all around us. I was in heaven. There I was, sitting between two naked girls, who then began to caress my legs and arms, laughing and having a good old time. I heard them talking, but I couldn't answer, my mouth felt as if it had been sewed up tight. Only in my head could I respond. I felt one of the girls trying to take off my bathing suit, and I didn't seem to have the mindset to stop her. I think it must have been Tracy because Sharon was beginning to whisper in my ear.

    "How does that feel?" she asked me, knowing full well the answer to her question. "You feel pretty good to me."

    "What the hell do you think your doing?" Francis screamed as if from far away. "Are you nuts?"

    I sort of saw a hazy Francis standing by the edge of the hot tub, but I was way too far gone to reply.

    "Enjoy yourself now, buddy, because when the B's hear about this." He stopped there, shaking his head and grinning from ear to ear.

    That was the last I saw of Francis that evening. Looking back on the whole thing, I realized that he was the tonic I needed to sober up. Ironic yes, but it was him that made me focus just enough to crawl out of the hot tub and call Beth to come and pick me up. I'm not too sure what happened after that. Beth found me walking around the employee's parking area, still damp and with most of my clothes in my hands. She told me later that I was completely incoherent when she asked me to explain what had happened. One thing I remember quite well was the look of utter disgust on her face when I first made eye contact with her, but the rest was a total blur.

Apparently, sweet, little Tracy put a tab of acid into my drink. I couldn't believe I had been slipped a mickey by an English girl! I hadn't been that high since my college days when I'd spend days going to Grateful Dead concerts. Eventually, Beth forgave me, especially since I was drugged and unwillingly detained. The fact that I was detained by a couple of naked girls made it a little harder for her to take but we worked through it. She knew that I never would have gone through with their plans for me. Of course, I had to insist that her body, despite two pregnancies, was much more attractive then their bodies. Why tell her that they were fit and trim when I didn't have to? I told her they were pale pudgy English girls who had eaten more than their share of Bangers and Mash. She bought it, I think. Who knows? Beth knows me better than anyone else in the world and probably saw through my story but forgave me anyway.

As I saw it, I got off easy. I've never stopped wondering what might have happened if Francis didn't show up when he did. Would I have played a part in an English threesome? Well … thankfully I escaped before the British did "come," and I'll leave it at that.

My real problem was with Francis and how he was planning on using this information. I decided my only option was to take a wait-and-see approach. I wanted him to lay his cards on the table first. That of course happened the second I came into the house the next day.

Michelle and Francis called me into the Mrs.'s office, the one that was adjacent to the mudroom. They were sitting there, happy as clams, waiting for me to arrive. You would have thought that they had hit the lottery by the way they were so content and pleased. As soon as I approached the desk where Francis was sitting, he gave me his ultimatum.

"Quit or be fired, take your pick." He was clearly enjoying the moment as he leaned back in the Mrs.'s chair, smoking her cigarettes. "As I see it you have no choice. If you quit it will save me the trouble of telling the B's about yesterday."

Michelle kept quiet, but I could tell that wild horses couldn't drag her away form the room. She was loving every minute of this.

Francis kept the pressure on. "So what will it be? Should I call Mrs. B now or not?"

"For what? I was drugged. I never would have gone into the hot tub if…"

I stopped short, knowing full well that it would be futile to try to convince these two of the truth.

"All I know is I that I saw you, naked," he continued, laughing at me along with Michelle. "You were naked with a couple of girls, drinking and doing drugs in Mr.'s private hot tub." He could hardly finish his sentence before falling into hysterics. "I am going to give you a couple of hours to think about it, but do me a favor and stay away from the hot tub."

Michelle and Francis were laughing their heads off. I, on the other hand, was not. I might not have a choice, I thought. The B's would never believe me over him, so I was screwed. I would never quit, though. It would be stupid because I would never receive unemployment benefits. But, if I were fired, there would be an unwanted blemish on my resume. I was in big trouble. Who could ever have imagined a scenario like this, being forced to make a decision because of this! It was absolute lunacy!

I didn't even want to stay for the party! How could I have got myself in such hot water?

As I saw it I had only one option, and that was to ask Andrew for some help.

Despite being prohibited anywhere in the house but the kitchen, I went up to his room to wake him up. The crew was sprawled out all over his large bedroom, lying on blankets and pillows around the floor. Andrew was in his bed with Megan sleeping rather peacefully. I tried nudging him but it was of no use, he was out cold. I needed to use louder tactics, I went right next to his ear and screamed at the top of my lungs, "WAKE UP!"

Andrew popped up suddenly, much to my satisfaction. He was barely coherent, but thankfully let himself be led out of the room.

I told him my situation and he seemed to find it slightly amusing. Despite being a pretty cool rich kid, the truth was, he didn't understand that money wasn't a given in my life like it was in his. He also didn't understand that the household servants playing a game of blackmail was actually quite serious for me. He didn't firmly grasp that this was my job, my occupation, and I needed to work. My mommy and daddy weren't going to fill my bank account as if it were a car low on gas. It took some background information on the entire situation for him to finally understand that Francis and Michelle weren't just screwing around with me, they wanted me gone. Andrew finally got it when he realized that his parents would find out about the party and his friends being at the house. He suddenly became the master of the house.

"Don't worry about a thing," he said, sobering up with each word. "Follow me." Andrew proceeded to pull his boxers up and head down the hallway.

I followed him as we went down the main staircase, and I realized this was actually the first time my chef clogs descended the gothic staircase.

We found the two novice extortionists conspiring in the breakfast room over a bagel and coffee. They were surprised to see Andrew up this early in the morning, but quickly knew the reason why when I meekly appeared out from behind him.

Andrew handled the situation magnificently. He matched their brand of coercion with some of his own. He kept it simple. If they were to rat on me, then he would be forced to tell his parents a few things, truthfulness not withstanding.

"Do I make myself clear?" he said to them after his mini-speech. "Good," he said quickly, not really allowing them to answer.

"Oh, by the way, Francis, take my car for a tune up, will you? And Michelle, I have a lot of laundry I need done. See to it for me." And off Andrew went, my knight in shining boxers, back up to resume his interrupted slumber.

Andrew and I never spoke about the day at the hot tub. In fact, what was once an easy relationship became strained and hard. I've always felt bad about that since he was a nice kid and all. I hope he has kept all his good traits since graduating college and getting on with his life.

CHAPTER NINETEEN

THE REST OF THE SUMMER TOOK A turn back to normalcy. (Well, I use the term normalcy, but nothing about that place was all too normal). Andrew jetted back to London, while my days of boredom and lack of human company continued as usual. We were informed by the B's of some changes in their plans. They were going to spend a couple more weeks in France and not return until the middle of September. For me that was the good news. The bad news was I had been volunteered to assist the banquet department in one of the nearby hotels owned by the Mr. They needed my assistance because of all the weddings that were booked for early September, and since the B's didn't need me to cook for them, they must have figured to get a little more mileage out of their personal chef and put me to another use.

The hotel I was assigned to sported the most modernized kitchen I had ever seen. They had all the equipment needed to turn out some pretty awesome meals. Despite it being such an incredible kitchen, a major problem existed in the form of the newly hired banquet chef. The hotel had recently hired this new, well-traveled banquet chef, who unfortunately couldn't cook his way out of a brown paper bag. It didn't take more than 20 minutes for me to figure that out. The chef (and I use that term loosely) was outfitted with both a decent-sized and semi-skilled crew. The only problem was that the crew only spoke Spanish, and the chef was experiencing some serious communication difficulties.

It was obvious the minute I walked into the kitchen that the chef disliked the fact that he was sent a helper, especially one he did not ask for, and therefore showed no excitement toward my mandated participation in his department. He reluctantly gave me a few menial choirs to do in hopes of keeping me busy and out of his way. First, I was given the job of peeling potatoes, then dicing **mirepoix** for soups.

Little did he realize that with the lack of complicated work, I was now in an easier position to survey the way he was doing his job. As I watched him pour a box of cornstarch straight into a pot of boiling gravy, hoping to thicken it without making the required slurry, I knew he was a shoemaker (a kitchen term for someone who doesn't know what the fuck they are doing). Considering the situation plus the fact that it wasn't my direct problem, I held my tongue. Hell, I wasn't getting paid enough to teach this guy how to cook. Besides, it didn't look like he would have been too open to my criticisms. I watched the jackass chef and his crew run around all day like chickens with their heads cut off, trying to get it together for a big function they had that night. A wedding with three hundred guests was on the books, and the menu seemed simple enough, assuming that it was being prepared by someone who had a clue. On top of all the botched cooking jobs, the head chef of the hotel was off that day so the success of the party was unfortunately up to this crack crew. I asked more than once if he needed any help but he kept finding inane jobs to keep me busy. I could see the storm brewing over the horizon, and I was just hoping it wouldn't turn out so bad. I was wrong. Hors d'oeuvre after hors d'oeuvre went out to the guests either burnt or undercooked. I sampled a pig in the blanket that still had a chill on it from the walk-in refrigerator and things spiraled downward from there. The salads were overdressed to the point of no return, the salty vinaigrette was dripping off the plates, and that was the highlight of the meal. Beef tenderloins resembling hockey pucks were sauced with goopy gravy that still had chunks of undiluted cornstarch floating through it. I will never forget the mushy, gray asparagus spears, the undercooked rounds of carrots, and the gluey, overwhipped mashed potatoes that accompanied the inedible meat.

As I helped plate up this atrocity and watched as the chef's sweat dripped from his paper chef's hat onto a few unlucky meals, I couldn't help thinking that some luckless father was flipping the bill for this meal from Alcatraz for his lovely daughter on this her special night. Some poor, badly informed man had signed on to have Dr. Frankenstein cook for his guests. Finally, the plate up for this disgusting meal was over. The slow torture finally came to an end, and I left without saying goodbye to the hack.

I didn't think much of it when I got home. I got there with just enough time to read my boys a story and kiss them goodnight. Beth and I were able to share a bottle of red wine and watch a movie not made by Disney before going to bed, which made it end up a great night for me.

At three o'clock in the morning, my phone rang, and my heart pounded in fear. Like any normal person, any time the phone rings that late I can't help think someone has died. This was one time I received news that was actually worse.

"What the hell happened tonight?" yelled an unknown voice.

"Huh, who's this?" I said, still half-asleep.

Beth was also sitting up and was pressing her ear to the phone trying to listen.

"I said what the hell happened tonight? I just got a call from my general manager saying that you fucked up an entire wedding!" the unknown voice shouted.

Beth backed away from the receiver, much more awake, her eyes wide with fright. The voice on the other end of the phone was loud and clear, and by this point I had a good idea who was yelling at me.

"Mr. B, is that you?" I asked, sounding quite quizzical.

"Who the hell do you think it is? And how could you fuck up a wedding so bad?" The Mr. continued. "My man tells me that the bride was hysterically crying that the food wasn't even edible! Are you trying to ruin me?"

"Are you kidding me?" I yelled back, getting angrier by the minute. "I did everything the chef asked me to do. And when I asked if he needed help he told me he had everything under control." I finally was able to get a word in by explaining I was just there and had nothing to do with it.

"If you were there, why didn't you fix it? What am I paying you for?" he asked a little more quietly.

My attempt to tell him the true version of the story fell on deaf ears. I don't think he cared either way; he was more upset about being called at the villa. He commanded me to report back to his house and to stay out of trouble until their trip was over. I hung up the phone and Beth came close to me and gave me a hug.

"You have to get out of that place," she pleaded, shaking her head in disgust. "Come on, let's go back to bed."

She urged me to lie back down and eventually rolled over into her normal sleeping position and was once more asleep. I tried to sleep but my ears were ringing with the Mr.'s booming voice. I didn't know what to do. I remained like that for hours, pondering my next move.

CHAPTER TWENTY

The B's returned as scheduled in the middle of September, and autumn was upon the city. My children were back in school, the summer was officially over, and so was the vacation for Francis and Michelle. I actually didn't mind the B's coming home—staring at the four walls in the kitchen for hours on end was starting to drive me crazy. Cooking for the dogs wasn't that taxing and I just couldn't find one more thing to clean.

The B's brought back pictures and stories of all the exciting things they did. Over and over I heard of all the wonderful meals they indulged in and how much they were forced to stuff themselves. The Mrs. had compiled lists and recipes from all different restaurants and put them in a binder and gave them to me right away to add to the house recipe box. The B's also brought back some tokens of appreciation for their employees. I received a small bottle of cologne. Nice yes, but a part of me couldn't help but be annoyed. Sure, this bottle of smelly French perfume would make up for being drugged, blackmailed, and almost divorced while they were gone. My whole crappy existence at the house was made so much better… gee, thanks, Mrs. B! After the fifteen-minute gift-giving session everything was back to normal, but I didn't think I could cope anymore.

I had been seriously contemplating finding another job ever since the 3 o'clock phone call Mr. gave me, but I just wasn't sure if I could handle going back to the restaurants or hotels. Beth had also suggested that she go back to work full time and I could just get a part-time job until I could find the right fit. But I was starting to think that there was no right fit for me. This place had been eroding my sense of pride for months and it was causing me to doubt my ability to make it someplace else. I was falling deeper and deeper into culinary depression.

With autumn finally there, I tried to look forward to some of the good things about this time of year, such as the beautiful foliage, the gentle fall breezes, and Halloween. Halloween was always a great holiday for the kids and me. I don't know of any child that doesn't get themselves into a frenzy with the prospects of filling their bags with loads of sweets, parading around street after street, house after house, while wearing clever costumes. You have to love a holiday that involves walking up to doors of people you don't even know and being rewarded for just our mere presence with candy and treats. It was a priority for me to have that night off. My kids would be crushed if I couldn't go out with them on their sugar hunt, and I would be crushed by not being with them.

Therefore, due to my boss's love of written correspondence, I decided to write up a formal declaration stating my need and desire for that night off, and I placed it on Mrs. B's desk in hopes she would grant my request.

Days and then weeks went by. The leaves changed colors and started dropping, making blankets of autumn colors on hidden streets and lawns. Carved pumpkins were out as well, along with scarecrows and all sorts of Halloween decorations. The B's, however, could care less about the holiday. They didn't even ask me to purchase any candy for them (or I should say Francis) to give out. They were candy scrooges. Their idea of celebrating All Hallows Eve was dining out at a four-star restaurant, and I had no problem with that, because this meant I could be home for some trick or treating, and possibly a little of both.

Mrs. B never got back to me on my request off, and I didn't have the guts to approach her on the subject. There was no chance she didn't see the note. It was just her way of torturing me. She probably knew all along that she and her husband would be dining out but had decided to wait and let me squirm until the last possible second.

It was about a quarter after five on October 31, 15 minutes before I could leave work. I was so excited that the thought of facing rush-hour traffic didn't bother me a bit. The countdown was on… 10 minutes to go, 5 minutes to go, 1 minute to go… I watched intently as the seconds ticked down to my final minute of bondage. And then, just as I left the kitchen, I heard Mrs. B on the speaker phone call out my name.

"Brian, Brian, are you there? Please pick up the phone," she yelled.

"Yes, Mrs. B," I said into the receiver.

"There has been a minor change of plans. I'm not really feeling up to going out to eat so we will be eating at home tonight," she said, faking sweetness. "You can just make us some veal chops or something."

I was heartbroken, crushed, a beaten man.

"Yes Mrs.," I reluctantly replied. I was even more reluctant to call Beth and tell her the sad news. When I did, she just about flipped out. She pleaded for me to tell the Mrs. that I made plans for the evening and I couldn't get out of them as easy as she got out of hers. Beth just didn't understand the power Mrs. B had. I was scared to death to say anything positive to her, and to say anything negative was simply not possible either. However, I only worked for Mrs. B, but Beth I had to live with, and besides, she was right. I knew deep down, somehow or some way, I had to confront the Mrs.

I called up to her room and she sounded annoyed that I dared to bother her .

"Yes, what do you want, I am lying down," she said.

I was mute for a minute.

"Yes, I'm waiting, what do you want?" she prompted, sounding sterner.

I told her about my Halloween plans, and I even embellished them a bit in hopes of encountering some form of mercy.

"Who's going to cook my dinner, then?" she asked.

I again told her about the plans I made.

"You see, since you told me you were going out for dinner, I made plans to be with my kids tonight and I just can't get out of it," I told her.

In my mind I could see all the other times she had done this to me and I was prepared to accept my unfortunate fate without complaint. To my huge surprise, she begrudgingly granted me permission to leave, all the while moaning about how she would now have to get dressed to go out and eat. I thanked her a few times and quickly ran to the laundry room to change out of my uniform. As I came out in my civilian garb, the Mr. was waiting for me and he was not too happy.

"When my wife tells you to do something, you better do it," he yelled.

Francis came in the mudroom just in time to see me get balled out.

"This will be the last time this happens," he stated, pointing viscously at my chest. His stubby finger actually made contact a few times as he screamed at me. I could smell the booze on his breath and it was obvious he was somewhat drunk. From the crazy look in his eyes, I felt that he hated my guts, and frankly, I hated his. It was a mutual hatred, and I left it at that, because I had to get home. I thought of my kids in their costumes, and of me being with them on a special night, giving them my full attention, something he and his wife never did with their kid. The thought of that made me feel a whole lot better.

Nothing was ever said about my decision to stick up for myself and leave that night. Mrs. probably wanted to imagine that it never happened and I doubt the Mr. even remembered anything that happened after his first bottle of scotch that day.

I only wished that I had been that strong a few weeks earlier when they didn't give me the Jewish New Year off. Rosh Hashanah was on a Wednesday that year, not my usual day off, and I kind of assumed the

Mr. would have, you know, shown a little respect. However, not only did they not give me the day off, they had me ask my wife to bake the traditional round challah bread for their dinner. I accidentally let it slip one day that my wife was a baker and ever since then they began asking me to have her bake them things. Beth was happy to do it because she thought it would make my life easier, but once again we got burned.

Thanksgiving came and went without incident. I worked during the day but the B.'s were off to one of their rival's, I mean friend's, houses for dinner. All the Mrs. asked me to do was make a couple of appetizers, no big deal, and I would be home in time for my family dinner. Well, of course things didn't turn out that way. Andrew came in for the weekend and slept all day Thursday. I didn't even know he was home. Around four o'clock that afternoon, the Mrs. called me on the intercom and informed me of Andrew being home, but that he would not be joining them at the friends' house for dinner and could I make him a hamburger.

It was not a problem, it's just that I had been sitting around the kitchen for three hours with nothing to do, waiting to go home. I could have made him whatever he wanted, but now I would be late to my in-laws and Beth was going to kill me.

I made Andrew his hamburger just the way he liked it with out ever seeing him. I left it in the warming oven and got the hell out of there. I made it to Beth's mom's house just in time for dessert, and the smile she gave me let me know that everything was all right.

CHAPTER TWENTY-ONE

THE WEEK AFTER THANKSGIVING, THE LOCAL WEATHER forecaster was predicting snow, and a lot of it. Winter wasn't officially here and already the threat of snow was paralyzing the region. The Mrs. had ordered that all household staple amounts needed to be doubled, the extra toilet paper alone needed a separate trip to the market. I almost had to call the department of transportation to get the amount of rock salt the Mrs. demanded.

The day of the predicted storm was upon us, and I had been trying all day to get out of there before the snow hit, but Mrs. B played her usual games with me by not telling me her plans for the evening. Late that afternoon Francis informed me that Mr. B needed to make up for his extended vacation by putting in a lot of extra working hours, and that he would be spending the night at the hotel to get in some early morning meetings. The impending snow storm was a large factor in his decision. And then the Mrs. had the brilliant idea of inviting a guest over for dinner. She wanted me to prepare pasta primavera and Caesar salad. I didn't think I was ever going to get out of there.

Before the Mrs.'s guest arrived, the snow had already started falling pretty hard. I heard the guest call the house when she reached the main gate. Francis buzzed her in and her BMW made it down the long driveway despite the snowy conditions I was very worried about the weather because my car sucked in any type of inclement weather.

The doorbell rang and I assumed Francis went to answer it. The Mrs. called down on the intercom to tell me to alert Francis that she would be down shortly and to get Mrs. B a drink. Mrs. B? I thought she was Mrs.

B... could there be another Mrs. B? Francis came back in the kitchen and I relayed to him the message.

"Who is this Mrs. B," I asked. I figured I had nothing to lose by asking him a question. Besides, curiosity was eating at me.

"She's the Mr.'s daughter-in-law from his old family," replied Francis, as if it was no big deal. "The Mrs. hates her, but once in a while she invites her over to show off the house. Now leave me alone." And with that, Francis left the kitchen to make her a drink.

I took a moment to spy on the visitor. I was rather intrigued by all this and had forgotten all about the storm outside. I looked through the small window of the swinging door that led out from the kitchen to the smallest of the dining rooms. The visitor's back was to me as I watched her take a drink from Francis and begin to look around at the artwork in the room. As she turned towards me, I got a good look at her face and my jaw fell to the floor. It was the lady from the grocery store. I wasn't sure what I was most surprised about—the fact that Mr. B's daughter-in-law was here or that she actually did her own grocery shopping. I turned away from the window to keep out of sight and bent down to look at her through the lower window. However, just as I peeked, she pushed through the door. The door hit me right in the face and knocked me ass first to the floor. I looked up as she looked down, and I could tell she recognized me as quickly as I had her. The lady from the supermarket was smiling down at me as she sipped her drink.

"Oh Samantha dear, there you are," my Mrs. B called out as she approached the kitchen. "What are you doing in here?" she asked, looking at both of us. Luckily I had gotten off my ass by that time.

"I see you have met my new chef. He is absolutely wonderful," Mrs. B said for purely self-indulgent reasons.

"Oh, absolutely wonderful, is he?" she said as she bit her lip, looking me straight in the eye.

"Come, let's catch up over dinner, shall we?" Mrs. B led Samantha out to the dining room.

Samantha was her name, and she was the Mr.'s daughter in law … I couldn't believe it. Meanwhile, the snow had continued to fall, so much so that I couldn't see out the kitchen window anymore, and I didn't know how I was going to get home that night.

The ladies ate their salads and pasta, and both decided to skip dessert. They polished off two bottles of wine, and Francis was opening up a third. My job for the night was over, so I ran out to my snow-covered car. There had to be at least ten inches of snow on the ground, and my car seemed completely immovable. I brushed off as much snow as I could and tried to back out of my spot, but the wheels were spinning, and I could barely see out of the windows. In minutes they were covered with snow again. I could see that this was pointless so I reluctantly got out of my car and headed back to the house. I told Francis my situation and he didn't seem all that surprised.

"We are stuck here, get used to it," he said.

He went to find the Mrs. and tell her that I was stuck there for the night, while I called Beth. She seemed relieved that I was going to stay there. She told me that the entire region was under a winter snow alert until late that night and said that she and the kids would be fine and would talk to me in the morning. Francis came back in the kitchen with a message from the Mrs. that I would be sleeping in one of the guestrooms.

It wasn't home, but it would surely do. There was a king sized bed, cable T.V., and my own bathroom. Josie brought me a pair of pajamas that looked brand new and said that they belonged to Andrew. I decided to relax with a hot bubble bath. It felt like I soaked for an hour in the oversized Jacuzzi tub. I couldn't get the fact that Samantha was the woman from the grocery store out of my head. She was so flirty that day and yet she was a married woman. For whatever the reason, she had certainly been on the prowl that afternoon.

After my relaxing bath, I rose and dried myself off. I turned on the heating light that was positioned on the ceiling and the bathroom got even toastier. I tied the towel around my hips and went into the dark bedroom. Apparently, Josie must have stopped in and turned out the lights, and I was pretty much blind. I reached onto the bed and tried to feel around for the remote control I had seen there earlier. A hand reached out and grabbed at me and caught on to my towel and with a tug it slipped off my body. I jumped away from the bed and felt around for the pajamas Josie had left for me. I had no idea what was going on… was I in the wrong bedroom, was I on candid camera? Had I just been punk'd?

"Come to bed, darling," Samantha purred from the bed.

"Listen, um, I'm very flattered by your interest, and you're very pretty but I'm married," I stammered as I fumbled in the dark trying to find the pajamas.

"So am I. Who cares?" she asked, as if she did stuff like this all the time.

I could not believe this was happening. Maybe my brain was fried from soaking in the tub too long. Things like this don't really happen in the real world, do they?

"Listen, Mrs. B, I…" And before I could execute my brilliant plan to escape, the real Mrs. B opened the door and flicked on the light.

"Oh my God, what is going on here?" she screamed at the top of her lungs.

Josie and Francis both came running to the room. There I was, caught, literally, with my pants down. I quickly grabbed the pajama bottoms and yanked them up, and I just stood there in total shock. Francis began to laugh, but a curt look from the Mrs. shut him up fast, then she turned her cold eyes onto me, pushed Josie and Francis out of the room and slammed the door behind her, leaving me alone with her half-naked daughter in-law.

"Alone at last," Samantha said.

"Are you crazy? Listen, lady, I want you out of here, now!" I hope I came across clearly enough for her.

She saw that I meant it and started to get out of the bed, and she made sure to move very slowly in an attempt to make me change my mind. But at that point I was so embarrassed that I didn't think I would ever be able to have sex or be naked in any bed ever again.

"I'll be right down the hall if you get lonely," she informed me as she finally left the room.

"Uh, yeah, thank you," I said, not truly believing the last 10 minutes of my life actually happened. Needless to say, I didn't get any sleep that night and remained fully clothed on top of the bed until I heard the snow plows on the street a while later. As soon as I did I got the hell out of that freak house.

That was the last time I ever saw Samantha. Even though I was afraid, I told Beth the story. She didn't know how to react at first, but she finally collapsed in a fit of laughter imagining my expression when everyone saw me buck naked. Beth had known me since college and knew how modest I was, and in a way she was proud of me for being faithful. If our marriage could survive that then I knew we had nothing to worry about for the rest of our lives.

I couldn't help but remain as embarrassed as all hell at work though, because the next day Francis told everybody what had happened. Michelle, especially, had more criticisms and comments to make than usual. Even the secretary had a joke or two to make at my expense. As for the Mrs., she never said a word.

CHAPTER TWENTY-TWO

That winter was as harsh a one as I could remember. As soon as one storm moved out another moved in. Like all billionaires, the thought of suffering through a full winter was out of the question, so the B's as usual intended to spend a chunk of it in sunny Hawaii. The only glitch for them was in having to celebrate the Christmas holidays a couple of weeks early. The birth of Jesus could surely be moved around to fit their schedule! I got out of cooking their Thanksgiving day dinner, but Christmas was their holiday to invite and excite, and there was much for all to do.

They celebrated the holiday much as most Christians do, despite the fact that Mr. B. was actually Jewish. (The Mrs. allowed him a tiny corner of the kitchen to light his menorah, but other than that not a latke or dradel could be found. I was the only other Jew in the place and it was a wild scene with just the two of us at the back counter in his giant mansion saying the blessings over the Hanukkah candles.)

Trying to explain the theatrics of their Christmas decorating would be very hard to do. If I was at Macys in New York City I could understand, but the amount of light bulbs and tinsel strewn around this property was downright obscene. An airport runway emitted less illumination than that electricity-draining monstrosity. As for the tree, imagine the fullest fir you've ever seen and then think about the most expensive and gaudy embellishments that could possibly be added, and then times that by one hundred. The tree was enormous, and the boxes and boxes of decorations that Francis carried up from the basement barely covered its numerous branches. Thankfully, the size of the tree was just big enough to cover the piles of gifts that were being put under it, most of them with Mrs. B's name attached to them. It was hard to imagine what this lady could possibly need, but from the looks of things under that tree, there still was plenty. It made me wonder if Mrs. B wrote to dear old Santa, to properly outline her wants for the holiday season. I could picture the Mrs. sitting at her desk, writing out her letter:

Dearest Mr. Claus,

Here's hoping the holiday season finds you and Mrs. Claus in fine spirits and health. If you would permit me, I would like to go over a couple minor discrepancies in last year's requests.

First, the diamond necklace. I really was expecting a bigger diamond in the center, one that would surpass in size the smaller ones that lined the rest of the necklace.

Secondly, the mink coat was supposed to be full length. I really didn't need another standard sized one. It really caused a problem for me because the dress I wanted to wear to the Mayor's dinner didn't look right underneath my other furs.

Finally, if you want to bring me chocolates, I prefer if they are dark chocolates. I just abhor milk chocolate.

As for this year, I really could use a new jet-black limousine. The white one just seems to get too dirty, and I really think I would look better coming out of a black one. Other than that, just my usual gifts will suffice. My New Year's resolution is to be a little less materialistic this year.

Merry Christmas

Mrs. B

For my part in their holiday, the B's posed to me a challenge. They wanted me to come up with a menu containing many of the traditional Christmas foods, but with an added element to distinguish the meal from all others they have ever had. This was the first time I was given even the remotest autonomy in creating a dinner party menu. I was sincerely shocked, but at the same time honored.

So I kicked some ideas around in my head for a while before coming up with what I believed to be an exciting but costly decision. Being that December is one of those special times of year when one of the most exotic of all culinary ingredients is in season, the idea for a White Truffle Christmas seemed like a good one to me. Very rarely have I had an opportunity to cook with this ingredient in the past, so to do a full dinner featuring them sounded rather thrilling. Most of the time, chefs are able to use only white truffle oil, or peelings, mainly due to their astronomical cost of about $150 dollars an ounce. I pitched the idea to Mr. B and he seemed intrigued by the premise, but of course he would have to consult his wife. Since the B's considered the Christmas feast to be their biggest event of the year, they were considerably excited about the thought of combining the truffle idea with their annual tradition. This was the 25th year that the B's hosted a dinner party in honor of the Winter solstice, Christopher Cringle, and everything this commercialized holiday has to offer, so what better way to show off then by pairing one of the most expensive ingredients in the world with their Christmas feast.

The B's were much more responsive than I could have ever anticipated. In fact, this was the first idea of mine that they showed any real human interest in. Normally, their responses to any off my dining options, whether they liked them or not, had been flaccid at best. Were the Christmas holidays numbing their faculties, or were the B's and I taking a first step toward a better relationship?

Selfishly, I was praying for the latter, mainly because of something I was told way back during my interview, almost one full year ago. I was so naïve back then. I had no legitimate frame of reference, yet I suffered from what I now know as false illusions about the reality of being a private chef; yet I endured the entire year for this one promise. I was praying for this one nugget of information to be true... this one promise that I've secretly kept to myself, a secret that Beth didn't know about. I would then be more than willing to go the extra step this Christmas dinner. This promise, in a lot of ways, had been the light at the end of the tunnel. Without this promise, it would have been entirely possible, if not probable, that I would have quit this job a long time ago. In my mind, I can still remember the B's last chef leaning over his desk, in an almost stealthy manner, and whispering, "The Christmas bonus will make it all worth while." Those were his exact words.

So, for me, this party's success could possibly add an extra 0 to the end of my bonus, and that would make my family's Christmas a hell of a lot happier.

The days preceding the grand event were closing in on us fast. The entire staff was still busy trying to put the finishing touches on everything. From the kitchen, I was able to quietly observe the mass confusion. It always puzzled me how one eve and one day could take so much preparation? The B's, while taking their preparation many steps farther, did in fact have the resources to do so. The Mrs. must have an entire section in her little black book which reads "Christmas help," because so many "Christmas experts" shuttled in and out of that place during the days before their party. They were the oddest assortment of representatives of the human race I had ever seen. Did it require a college degree to consult in tree decorating? I'm sure the guy who told me he was the foremost expert on tinsel designing really needed that 4-year program, taught by the esteemed Mrs. Claus at NPU (North Pole University). Or how about the lady who came in the kitchen and asked why I used pink sugar for Rudolph's nose and not the traditional red on my Christmas reindeers. I wasn't quite sure, especially since I was just a good Jewish boy, but I thought the penalty for bastardizing an innocent cookie hadn't been charged in many years. I think the last time someone had perpetrated such a crime was during the long ago "Great

Cookie Caper", led by the vicious and furry blue Cookie Monster. I could see it all so clearly, my guilty face plastered in every post office this side of Sesame Street with a large reward for my capture. So, like any good criminal, I admitted to the lady that I was wrong, and never again would I desecrate something so holy, so godly, and so sacred as a Christmas Cookie.

The rest of the Mrs.'s collection of holiday helpers wound up being no less pretentious than the last two, but the B's definitely got there moneys worth from these North Pole rejects. Nothing was overlooked, not one poinsettia was out of place, not one sheep went astray in any manger scene. They even altered the phone ringer to play assorted Christmas carols. I was just relieved that the majority of my role in this holiday production was almost completely free from any of their scrutiny, all except for that one run-in with the dreaded Cookie Gestapo.

The day the courier brought the imported white truffles all the way from Italy, the B's made far less then a modest display of excitement. Each one was carefully taken out from its wooden container, and fully scrutinized. They were examined, felt, smelt, and just about prayed to, not even the dogs got that excited when I gave them their treats. I guess when you're shelling out a few thousand dollars, the right to fawn over anything, even fungi, couldn't be that unjustified. Hell, my buddies and I spend a few dollars for a pizza and a case of beer and we can hardly contain ourselves.

It only took me only an hour or so in the company of the truffles and I was able to compile an entire menu. It was an ode to the white truffle, but at the same time blended elements with the B's traditional Christmas favorites. It was intriguing how just one whiff of the truffles could excite both the consumers and stoke a chef's creative fire like no other ingredient on earth. Reading over the menu, I felt very pleased, and had no reservations in giving it to the B's for final approval. The menu was officially approved.

Christmas a la White Truffle

1st Course
Scallop "White Tie"

2nd Course
Baby greens, Quail egg, Truffle Vinaigrette

3rd Course
Bass, Brandade, Fried Parsley

4th Course
Chestnut crusted Venison, Potato Gratin

Sides
Spaghetti Squash, Roast Sweet Potato, Baby Vegetables

5th Course
Dessert Buffet Featuring
White Chocolate Truffles
Pumpkin Pie
Miniature Frozen Grand Marnier Soufflé
Warm Apple Fritters, Rum Raisin Ice cream
Spiced Poached Pears, Brandy Ginger Snaps
Christmas Cookies
Chocolates

The night was finally upon us. All the planning, the hard work, and all the expectations were finally coming to fruition. But this time, the B's were completely removed from what was happening behind the scenes. It was now the responsibility of their staff to make it all happen.

The B's were busy frolicking with their friends and family. This party had a much different tone to it than any of the others they had the past year. There was way less tension in the air; a feeling of serenity was ushered in along with the holiday season. A white Christmas was granted to us, and even the normal everyday hatred between enemies was put on the back burner. Michelle, Francis, and I called a momentary truce, at least till the B's left for Hawaii. We all had something to gain by being on our best behavior, and there would be plenty of time to make up for our current considerations.

Maybe, I thought, I had this whole private chef business wrong. At first, I didn't know what to really expect, and then for months on end I learned to expect only the worst, but now? Maybe I was just feeling sappy from under a veil of holiday cheer, but perhaps one holiday could make all wrongs be right. Could the promise of a fat man in a red suit, Frosty the Snowman, and a partridge in a pear tree bring peace on earth, or at least to the B's house? Could it mean the end to oppression, and possibly even mend the tears in this place's fabric? Only time could really answer my questions, but for now I was feeling pretty good about my situation. The promise of a Christmas bonus certainly did not hurt matters.

CHAPTER TWENTY-THREE

The dinner was progressing without a hitch. Classical versions of Christmas tunes were softly echoing into the kitchen. Things were feeling so surreal, with Francis actually helping tray up the hors d' oeuvre's instead of laughing at them. He even tried one without spiting it back out. This certainly had the makings of a night to remember.

One after another, the courses entered the dining room with much anticipation. The guests were going crazy over the excessive amounts of white truffles being sliced tableside onto their plates. Francis went around the table, shaving the truffles with a special device, designed for just that purpose. Slice after slice fell gently through the air landing delicately, much like snowflakes, on every plate.

The first course was a hit. The seared scallop, layered with foie gras, Swiss chard, and white truffle, was baked in a shell of pastry dough and then placed upon a nappe of Port wine sauce.

Next came the tender baby greens which were tossed in a truffle dressing, with two pan-fried quail eggs encased in fluted circles of brioche, leaned gently against the completed salad.

The fish course was a seared filet of striped bass laying atop a petite cake of brandade. Parsley leaves, fried to a forest green, were positioned around the plate. A drizzle of white truffle oil perfumed the fish, and I could smell the aromas from the plates long after Francis carried them into the dining room.

The main course was sublime. A chestnut-encrusted venison chop was paired perfectly with the creamy, truffled potatoes. A light lingonberry sauce and sprig of thyme completed the dish.

The dessert buffet was a sweet tooth's heaven, a myriad of mouth-watering temptations filling two skirted 10-foot-long tables. Besides all the items I prepared, some of the guests also brought some tasty treats. A traditional Yule log, a Black Forest cake, and a coconut cream pie only added to the already grandiose spread.

The B's and their guests drank and consumed like there was no tomorrow. So much so, I was wondering when the B's were going to get around to spreading some holiday cheer in my direction. I hoped they wouldn't forget about little old me, despite all the ado going on at the party. Francis noticed me acting a bit antsy; my pacing back and forth from the laundry room to the kitchen was a dead giveaway.

"What's wrong with you?" he asked.

"Oh, I'm just wondering, well, I'm just waiting to see how they liked everything," I answered

"Please. Give me a break. You're not waiting for no pat on the back," he laughed.

"Well, I…" I didn't know what to say.

"Well, nothing," he interrupted. "You're waiting for your bullshit bonus, aren't you?" He exclaimed. "You don't think its anything special, do you?" he asked incredulously. "You do, don't you? You poor sucker, you think…" he paused. "You think, oh my god, you are such a sucker!" He shook his head in disbelief.

"What, did you think that they were going to break the bank for you?" Francis asked when I remained silent.

He must have read the disappointed look upon my face, but I knew he had to be wrong. Maybe his bonus would be nothing special, but mine? Mine had to be, all of those extra hours of work, staying late, coming in early had to pay off.

"We'll see," I said, trying to sound confident.

"No, we won't see anything, you'll see," he said laughing.

Francis left the kitchen to tend to things in the main family room.

The B's and their guest were singing Christmas carols around the tree, drinking and having a good old time. I was starting to get a little nervous at this point. Francis had to be pulling my leg for old time's sake. He is such an instigator, I thought to myself.

Finally, the swinging door opened, and a red-faced and stumbling Mr. B appeared before me. He could hardly walk a straight line, and barely stopped short of bumping into the kitchen island. He reached into his jacket pocket, and pulled out an envelope. Then he attempted to speak.

"Brian, Brian, you've been here cooking here for a while nows," he slurred heavily. "The Mrs. and I's have something for you. Merry Christmas." Then he handed me the envelope.

"Thank you, thank you very much," I said, trying without much luck to shake his hand.

Afterwards, Mr. B stumbled back from where he came and I ran into the laundry room and slammed the door behind me. I sat down on a few cases of Snapple and stared down at the envelope. It was a plain white envelope, no name or anything, but I didn't care, it was what was on the inside that counted. Carefully, I opened the envelope, so as not to damage any of the contents. It looked like a check. Oh yes it was a check. A check, written out in my name. A check written out in my name for ... fifty bucks. Fifty bucks? Fifty fucking bucks! That couldn't be right. I looked back into the envelope for some missed bills or something. Something! There had to be something I missed! But there wasn't something, there wasn't anything else, just the check. Not even a fucking membership in the Jelly of the Month club.

For a lousy fifty bucks, I spent a whole year kissing ass, a whole year of sucking up, a whole year of feeling like a total loser, for fifty extra dollars. I kept repeating, over and over in my head, fifty extra dollars, fifty extra dollars, fifty extra dollars ...

Methodically, I walked into the kitchen. I tore out a piece of paper from my notebook and proceeded to sit down. I reached for a pen from my jacket pocket and began to write.

Mr. and Mrs. B,

I am officially informing you, as of this very second, I will no longer serve under your employment. My one year sentence in your prison like mansion has ended. My New Year's resolution of lessening the mental torture in my life will begin a few days early. I have had enough. It is with my last shred of respect, my last scrap of personal pride that I write this letter in hopes of expressing to you, with all my heart and soul, that you can take your fifty dollars, your job, and all of Mrs. B's suppositories and shove them straight up your ass.

Free at last,
Brian

CHAPTER TWENTY-FOUR

I stabbed the note with a pairing knife and attached it eye-level onto a cupboard door. As I stood back to take in the moment, it dawned on me that this letter wasn't just written for my benefit. It was written on behalf of every other maltreated member of the culinary profession that had ever been in a similar situation and never got the opportunity to express their feelings. This letter was a symbol to every father who missed his sons' sporting events, every mother who had to work a Mother's Day brunch, and every boyfriend or girlfriend who had to work nights, weekends, and holidays away from their loved ones. A lifetime of regret poured out of me in that letter and I regretted not a word.

So there it hung, my letter of resignation, expressing my sorrow and contempt and the fifty-dollar check. If that was all they could spare then I figured that they needed it more than I did.

I left their house for the last time, with nothing more than I came with, except some harsh insights on the life of a private chef. Of course, not every private chef position can be painted with the same brush, but I would seriously have to be much more inquisitive if I was ever again to pursue a job of this nature. But more importantly, it's not the job, rather the people that I would work for, about whom I would be more selective. However, this I swear: I will never, ever again stand in line at a grocery store to buy freaking tampons, that's for damn sure!

I arrived home that night and wrapped myself in the protective cocoon of my family and stayed there for the rest of the year. I needed that few weeks off to recuperate and decompress from my ordeal and it made all the difference in the world. I emerged wiser than before. That place hadn't killed me, it only made me stronger. My self-esteem wasn't shot to hell; it was just in better perspective after being temporarily on hiatus. I knew I needed to find a place that valued family and personal time off as much as they valued a chef's skills and work ethic. And I eventually found a company that allowed me to work hard and yet have a life outside the kitchen.

As for the B's, they had Francis call my house a couple of times when they got back from Hawaii in attempts of getting me back but I was never able to speak to any of them again, and Beth simply answered for me that I had moved on.

The truth is that I am a chef, and a chef I must be. I was born to cook, and nothing or nobody can deter my passion for doing what I truly love to do. Some people might be able to choose their line of work and others may follow in their parent's footsteps, and some others may even choose their jobs merely on the basis of salary, status, or glamour. For me, well, I never had a choice. The passion to cook is engrained in me, and turning my back on it would be as futile as trying to remove my soul. Despite all the ups and downs of this crazy profession, I wouldn't want it any other way.

I think back on that fateful day long ago when I got my reading done. From this moment forward, the tarot card depicting the Queen of Cups upside down will always remind me of Mrs. B, and it is one card I would prefer never to encounter again.

The End

A NOTE TO READERS

The author has been working as a chef for over 13 years, and has served time in the restaurant business for over 20 years. This book is a work of fiction, and no one family, restaurant, or hotel is portrayed in this book. Names and characters are the product of the author's imagination. Any resemblance to actual people or places is purely coincidental. Although some real restaurants, people/celebrities, and the like are mentioned, all are used with the best of intentions.

The Author would like to thank Aaron for being the first guinea pig and a big thanks to Kathy for all of her help; this book would not have been possible without you.

GLOSSARY

Al Dente – firm to the bite. Basically, not raw or not over cooked.

Arepas – a Colombian and Venezuelan food item made with cooked corn flour, water, and salt; then fried on a griddle. Tastes a lot better than it sounds.

Birkenstocks – comfortable kitchen clogs, all pretentious chefs wear them.

Beurre Blanc– Fr. For white butter, a sauce made with shallots, white wine and butter. A super fattening French sauce.

Blanching – cooking food very quickly in boiling water. Like watching your vegetables on High Definition T.V.

Blini – leavened Russian pancake made with buckwheat flour. Blini is plural for blin.

Bolognese – an Italian meat sauce for pasta. My sons know it as American chop suey.

Brandade – French dish of a puree made with salt cod, olive oil, and milk. The Italians call their salt cod Bacalao, if you care to know.

Brioche – a French bread made with eggs and butter. I call it Challah.

Brunoise – cut of approx. 1/8 inch. Cutest little squares you've ever seen.

Calamata Olives – a larger sized black olive from Greece. Zeus's favorite.

Capers – closed flower buds of a shrub native to the Mediterranean, they are cured in salted vinegar and develop a salty – sour flavor. Under used commodities.

Chef's Knife - see French knife.

Chiffonade – to finely slice herbs or leafy greens. Taco lettuce.

Chinese Mandoline – a manually operated slicer. Makes cool waffle cut potato chips.

Concassee – peeled, seeded and diced tomatoes. Also see Monder.

Consommé – Fr. For rich broth that has been clarified. A clear broth that costs a lot more money than soup.

Coulis - sauce made from the puree of vegetables or fruits. Fancy name for sauce.

Crème Anglaise – a rich French custard sauce made with eggs, sugar, cream, and vanilla. A.k.a. vanilla sauce.

Crème Fraiche – a cultured cream product, has a tangy flavor; the French love it. A.k.a. sour cream.

Demi-Glace – Fr. for half glaze. A brown sauce reduced by at least half.

Emulsion – uniform mixture of unmixable liquids by use of blender or egg yolk. Ingredients at war temporarily make friends.

Flambe - food that is flamed by liquor. Keep a fire extinguisher handy.

Foie Gras – the enlarged liver of a duck or goose. The birds are forced fed and kept on a corn diet. Reference the movie "Seven", and check out the gluttony part; then you will have an idea on what the birds are going through.

Food Mill – a tool for pureeing foods through a perforated disk by a hand crank. A real pain in the ass to clean.

Frenched – to remove the meat from the top of bones. A sexy way to serve chops.

French Knife – see Chef's Knife.

Frisee – a variety of endive with green curly leaves. The lettuce that doesn't comb its hair.

Haricot Vert – Fr. For green beans, thin green beans with small seeds. Those damn French have a different word for everything.

Knead – to work dough with your hands or by mixer. Hell, technically you could even use your feet.

Lemon Grass – tropical grass from South East Asia, with long greenish stalks and a strong lemon flavor. Smells like lemon, tastes like lemon, but not a lemon.

Lingonberry – a relative of the cranberry. Has a red skin and a tart flavor. One of the more under-appreciated members of the berry family.

Lola Rosa – small tender salad green, curly and reddish. A very pretty name.

Mache – also known as Lamb's lettuce, very delicate dark green leaves. Baaa.

Monder – the act of skinning and seeding a tomato.

Nicoise – a salad from Nice, France. Are people from Nice Nice?

Oxacaan – region of Mexico. Hard word to spell and pronounce.

Paillard – a pounded piece of meat or poultry; usually grilled. If no kitchen mallet is available don't worry, a wine bottle can do the trick.

Pate Brisee – Fr. For a rich, flaky short dough used as a crust for sweet and savory. A gourmet term for pie dough.

Patty Pans – a small yellow or green squash that has a fluted exterior. You're mostly paying for appearance, usually better off with just a summer squash.

Peel – a wooden tool with a long handle to transfer bread or pizza in and out of the oven. A really big spatula.

Primavera – Italian for springtime and used to describe dishes with lots of vegetables. What, there's no vegetables during the other seasons in Italy?

Proof – to allow yeast dough products to rise before baking. There are actually boxes made just to proof in.

Prosciutto – Italian ham that is seasoned, salt cured, and air-dried. Try a few slices of this on your next hoagie.

Radicchio – a variety of Chicory from Italy. Purple and white in color, a tad bitter. Let's face it, a green used mostly for color.

Raft– a mass of ground meat, minced vegetables, egg whites, and the stock's caught impurities. The clarification process causes these impurities to rise to the top of the simmering pot and get caught in this raft. Not for pool use.

Ramekin – a small ceramic dish. Fancy name for a little Pyrex.

Red Oak/Green Oak – a leaf lettuce. Why yes, of course it looks like Oak tree leaves.

Roesti – a cake made from shredded potatoes and then fried. A big fat latke.

Roulade – something rolled and stuffed. Jelly rolls are technically roulades.

Sear – to brown food quickly over very high heat. Not burn, but SEAR.

Shoe Maker – a fixer of shoes. A kitchen hack, a nickname for a cook or chef who sucks.

Slurry – mixture of starch and cold water, used for thickening. A godsend for Chinese food.

Star Anise – a dried star-shaped spice from China. It has a licorice flavor and makes up a part of the Chinese five-spice powder. I love these in braised duck.

Toque – a tall white pleated hat. The official headgear for chefs.

Truffle – a black or white fungus that grows underground, near the roots of trees. A round and various smaller sized item that has a tough and wrinkled exterior. Trained dogs from expensive French schools unearth these smelly things so rich and famous people can consume them.

Trussing – to secure an item by using string. Helps the item retain its shape during cooking. To put a bird in bondage.

Turbot – a flatfish found in the Atlantic Ocean and the Mediterranean Sea. It has a delicate flavor and firm white flesh. I think Jesus caught a couple of these beauties on the Sea of Galilee.

Yukon Gold Potatoes – a slightly round spud with a waxy yellow skin. Great for mash potatoes or sautéing. Idahos got nothing on these guys.

ISBN 1-41205743-4